10 STACKS TO SUCCESS

Jerome "Jay" Isip

10 Stacks to Success: How to Achieve Success One Goal at a Time

Published by: Jerome J Isip

Disclaimer

All Scripture quotations are taken from Bible in Basic English Version of the Bible.

Cover Illustration Copyright © 2014 by Jerome "Jay" Isip

Cover design by Robyn Mendolla LLC

Book design and production by DocUmeantDesigns.com

Editing by Gloria Herrera and Timothy Hands

Chapter opening illustrations Robyn Mendolla LLC

Author photograph by Robyn Mendolla LLC

First Edition, 2014

Published in the United States of America

ISBN13: 978-1502960269
ISBN-10: 1502960265

Dedication

This book is dedicated to everyone from Belleville, New Jersey

Contents

Dedication iii

Acknowledgements vii

Introduction ix

Stack 1: Foundation 1

Stack 2: Positive Attraction 11

Stack 3: Behavior 27

Stack 4: Dream a Little Dream 39

Stack 5: Surroundings 53

Stack 6: Fight the Fear 63

Stack 7: Money 73

Stack 8: Creativity. 87

Stack 9: Actions. 99

Stack 10: Experience 113

References 131

Introduction

10 Stacks to Success: How to achieve success one goal at a time is a simple guide with powerful content intended to help others create a successful lifestyle and achieve their goals in life through proven tactics.

Topics include:

✓ Building a strong mental and physical foundation.

✓ Producing a positive, productive mindset.

✓ How to defeat our mental fears.

✓ How to unlock creativity.

✓ And finally, how to earn a substantial amount of money in order to enhance your lifestyle

Using in-your-face facts, observations many ignore, vividly entertaining examples, and extensive research and knowledge from many of the elite icons in the life-success field, readers will develop a new perspective towards achieving success. While your head may spin faster than a Hanukkah dreidel and the tactics may come across as "crazy", this book is designed to make your brain view life in new light, unleashing the amazing person inside.

The decisions we make now are decisions that will either take us one step further from our goals or one step closer. The decision, you see, is all yours.

This was my life altering decision:

In 2001, after repeating senior year, I finally graduated high school. While I wasn't sure what I wanted to do, I knew that several more years of schooling wasn't my priority. However, my parents forced me to attend community college. My father proudly drove me to fill out the application, as he believed this was the beginning of a bright future for me. I sluggishly sharpened my No. 2 pencil and slowly began to fill the circle next to "Asian." Minutes later, after completing the application with absolute disgust, fear, and anxiety, I begrudgingly slid it under the plexiglass window towards the female attendant who seemingly hated her job. She then proceeded to muffle through the intercom "That'll be fifty-five dollars. Cash, check, or credit?" She snapped her bubble gum multiple times. I slowly handed her my check filled out in the blood from my fingertips and watched her take my soul with nine-inch nails that were more decorated than a Christmas tree.

A month later, I received a notification letter with the return address "666 Lucifer Blvd." My final payment with the devil was scheduled on Monday November 4th at 8:30 a.m., the date of my placement exam. With overwhelming joy and a smile stretching ear to ear, my mother proudly took the letter and hung it on the refrigerator for all to see. To celebrate this proud "decision" of my attending college, my parents promised me (in their best Bob Barker voice) a BRAND NEW CAR!

That fateful Monday morning, November 4th, finally arrived. I tensely walked into the classroom with eyes wider than a porcelain doll and looked at the "teacher" tasked with officiating the test. At 8:30 a.m. sharp I began filling out the top portion of the test. My body was in complete discomfort and my nerves trembled enough to sound off the car alarms in the parking lot. Just after writing in my name, I stared at the drop ceiling and found myself enveloped in a daydream about what life would be like if I went through this experience. I saw myself constantly taking tests, studying pointless information, and sharing unoriginal ideas with other students. All I could visualize was a life that was being created, controlled, and manipulated by someone else. I snapped out of this Freddy Krueger-esque nightmare only to realize I was sweating and panting like a fat kid in gym class. I immediately stood up, authoritatively stomped to the front of the room and handed in my test to the Bride of Chucky (the teacher). She immediately asked me, "Are you sure you are finished?" I confidently responded, "Yes. I am sure." As this woman stared at the blank test sheets in front of her, she peered back at me and replied, "You know this is your future, right?" With a confident smile (and a giggle) I responded, "Naaahh, this is your future!" I pointed my finger around the classroom and at her face. The entire classroom erupted in laughter, cheered, and applauded as I exited the room (at least that is how I remember it.) Monday, November 4th at 8:33 a.m. I made the intuitive, fearless, confident, and positive decision that changed my life for the better and forever. I chose to create my own dreams.

So what is your dream? What is holding you back from living an extraordinary life? What is keeping that amazing person locked inside? What is it after all, that you really want? The answer is in the palm of your hands.

Use this guide to achieve your dreams of success. A new journey to live your dream can begin at this very moment. The decision for enlightenment, abundance, and happiness can only be decided by you. What will you decide?

STACK 1

FOUNDATION

"The foundation stones for a balanced success are honesty, character, integrity, faith, love and loyalty."
—Zig Zigler

For thousands and thousands of years, humankind has built many memorable works of art that continue to be appreciated today for all of their beauty. Through wars, riots, thieves, earthquakes, and storms, the Colosseum of Italy, the Pyramids of Egypt, the Acropolis of Athens, Greece, the Chichen Itza Ruins of Mexico, the Konark Sun Temple of India, and the Great Wall of China are among the many breathtaking sights that are still standing today. Yet, why is it that many other extravagant achievements of man have crumbled over the years and now cease to exist? Why is it that the Pyramids of Giza still stand today as the last of the Seven Wonders of the World? Why did the later pyramids not last as long? Was it because of the many wars the land saw or was it simply an act of time? Well, maybe the fault lies inside of the foundation. Centuries ago, men across the world developed their own individual system where they imagined something great and strategically placed each stone accordingly. Due to their logic, determination, and willpower, they all achieved something spectacular that thousands of years later still stands strong because they knew that foundation was paramount to structure. So, it would seem the early Egyptians had it right: If we build a strong foundation, our legacies will last a lifetime.

If we are seeking self-improvement, then it is a no-brainer that we must reconstruct the foundations within ourselves. In order to move forward, we must be willing to change our behavior, habits, and current lifestyle for the better. Time after time, we witness people trying to change their foundations, but they give up way too quickly. They start with the motivation and will to create a better person and suddenly, the motivation wears off and they are right back where they started. They make the New Year's resolution to go to the gym, go for a solid week, maybe two, and slowly but surely, the days at the gym begin to dwindle. Before you know it, they are heavier than before they started, tossing around the "I'll start on Monday" excuse as they sit in front of the TV with a pint of Ben & Jerry's. I am sure we have all been guilty of using this excuse, but how many times has it worked? Then there are those who start to set a budget limit on expenses to save money. A solid month of hard saving goes by and the "I have been good for a month, I deserve a night out" excuse comes out and next thing you know, their entire savings was blown in one night at the bar from downing Vodka and Diet Cokes because they also happened to be "watching their calories." Come on people! Realize that these are common lies that haunt all of us. Realize that we constantly convince ourselves that we "deserve" a break from the hard work we have put in while building a new foundation when in reality, we have barely put down the soil.

In order to build a new, more solid foundation we need to be willing, determined, patient, persistent, and, most importantly, honest with ourselves. You cannot put down the floor of a house unless the soil is leveled correctly.

You cannot ice a cake until the batter has baked to a firm consistency. You cannot place a boxer inside the ring until he or she has properly trained. You cannot throw a fat kid on a tricycle and expect it to reach ultimate velocity—it is just going to break down! It will break down just like we will if we fail to build solid ground within ourselves. A strong, sturdy, and stable foundation is the first step in self-improvement.

How do we start? Right here, right now. At this very instant, we must decide what structure we want to build because it will be the key to everything. We cannot start building and creating self-improvement if we do not have a plan or a thought process—a structure.

Here are some key factors that can help build a strong foundation:

- *Organization*—Being organized is not just a physical quality, but also a mental one. How many times have we had a great idea or thought about something and then said to ourselves *"Yeah, I'll remember to do that"* and then completely forgot? Exactly, we *always* forgot. Keeping our thoughts organized will lead to organized action. How do we keep our thoughts organized? Are you ready for the big case-cracker? WRITE THAT S%!T

DOWN! Make a daily list of targeted accomplishments, daily thoughts, future activities and goals
and carry it with you. In doing so, you will never forget what is needed to do or what thought
popped into your head on a specific day because
you will be able to reach into your pocket, purse,
or fanny pack and look at your list or write down a
new idea or thought. Totally mind-blowing, huh?
But it doesn't stop there. Once the daily list has
been created, let us take it a step further like the
big boys that we are and cross out each task that
has been accomplished. Trust me when I say that
this small action will change your life. Personally,
I format my daily lists to be geared towards a goal,
big or small, and write down the tasks that will get
me closer to that specific goal. I personally enjoy
making sure my daily tasks are different from the
day before so that I am accomplishing one mini
goal at a time and changing my normal routine.

- *Change the route*—When was the last time you
  did something for the very first time? Be aware of
  your normal activities and change them because
  what we are doing in the present has yet to change
  our future if we are still in the same position as the
  past. Realize that to achieve something different,
  we must do something different. If we are geared
  towards performing the same daily routine, can
  you guess what is going to happen? Absolutely
  <u>nothing</u>. Following the same routine will only set
  us up to accomplish nothing and will display the
  same exact results we have continually received.

- *Productive Establishments*—Establishing specific activities to perform daily will help us progress towards our goals. We have to promise ourselves to repeat these daily rituals in order to keep us focused on changing our routine. Establishing a specific task at a specific time and location is the most beneficial way to ensure that these activities are completed successfully. I have learned that the best time to establish these activities is first thing in the morning. Before we check our phones, before we go on Instagram and Facebook, or before we light up that first roach or stogy. I mean if you have to piss or drop a deuce than that is your first doodie . . . I mean duty (daa dumm ching!). Here are some examples of productive activities that can be done consistently:

  o Do 100 jumping jacks.

  o Read a motivational chapter or article to get you inspired.

  o Make a list of things and people you are grateful for.

  o Play your favorite song and shake what yo mama gave ya!

Realize that any productive activity will help boost the day in the correct direction and bring joy to our lives first thing in the morning. It will get our blood moving and brains working so that we are physically and mentally prepared to enter the day with a positive attitude.

- *Get fit you lazy bum*—As mentioned before, we need a strong mental and physical foundation to progress. Taking care of our bodies is equally important as our minds. Therefore, you cannot change one without the other. They are both meant to complement each other through the process of positively changing the foundation in ourselves. Now, I am not saying we must become as chiseled as a Michelangelo sculpture (even though that would be nice), but we must realize that our health is a very important part of our progression. The better we take care of our health, the better our lives will progress.

Physical changes to consider:

o Eating clean and having a healthy diet.

o Joining a group training gym (KRANKSYS-TEMS.com, check them out).

o Going for jogs or lifting weights as part of a daily routine.

o Quitting drinking alcohol and smoking cigarettes.

o Taking up kickboxing or Brazilian ju-jitsu.

o Not eating that 10th cookie with a side of Yoo-hoo spiked with a little rum.

By being healthier, we are creating a clearer picture in our minds by providing our bodies with the energy needed to go after our goals each day. Give the body that extra boost by feeding it with the proper vitamins and minerals. Use that Monday-Sunday pill case that has been sitting in your drawer collecting dust if you must! Understand that when we fuel the body correctly, our minds and bodies will adapt to being geared only in the right direction. You cannot fill a 1995 Honda Civic with diesel fuel, try to start it in -13 degree weather, and expect to drive from New Jersey to California. Do you catch my Tokyo drift, bro? (Do you understand my example, sir or madam?) Only by having the proper engine build (mind), a durable and comfortable exterior design (body), and the proper fuel intake (health/soul) will we be ready for the journey ahead of us.

Personal Activity #1: Let us start by eliminating our non-productive activities and replacing them with something productive towards our goals. I am sure there are

PLENTY of things we could eliminate and replace to start changing our foundation. Here are some examples:

- **Useless Activities:**

    o Watching Jersey Shore, The Real Housewives, Eyewitness News, and Dr. Oz.

    o Ordering pepperoni pizza for lunch 5 times a week.

    o Opening the Star Ledger only to read about a 17-year-old Puerto Rican that robbed a candy store using a Snickers-Bar to pose as a gun.

    o Drinking at Happy Hour and ordering a "WAMBURGER[1]" to eat with the rest of the Complainasorus[2].

- *Useful Activity Replacement:*

    o Replacing TV with exercise. Go for Jog, a walk, do some push up and sit ups.

    o Replacing pizza with a good healthy salad or sandwich for lunch.

    o Replacing the newspaper with an inspirational book or article.

    o Hang out with people who motivate you by sharing positive ideas. Reach out to someone

---

1   Wamburger—food that is consumed by people who complain
2   Complainasorus—a group of people who share negative stories and complaints

who is successful (in your own perspective) and have a "sit down" (i.e. meeting) with them.

_____

_____

_____

_____

_____

_____

_____

_____

GET READY TO RUMBLE

Time to walk the walk and talk the talk, folks. Now that we have a better idea on how to begin creating a foundation, or more importantly, the importance of a foundation, it is time to take some action. We need to stop putting our progressive thoughts on the back burner and start building on them now. Do we want positive changes in our lives? Do we want to enhance our income astronomically? Do we want to activate the amazing human being that is inside us all? Then stop "ugh'ing" around and dragging your feet on the floor! Stop feeling sorry for yourself, get off your ass, and do something productive! Let us all start by celebrating the decision to start a new life and enjoy the damn journey!

STACK 2

POSITIVE ATTRACTION

"I attract to my life whatever I give my Attention, Energy and Focus to. Whether positive or negative."—Michael Losier

Part of building a new foundation is learning to attract what we wish to have in our new positive life. As such, we must develop the correct mental attitude and fill it with characteristics such as faith, integrity, hope, optimism, courage, generosity, tolerance, tact, kindness, and common sense.

We are not what we say we are because nobody is content anymore with just being his/herself. In today's world, we are all too busy labeling ourselves or trying to find the right way to label what we know as "things." These "things" are the roles we play on a daily basis such as occupations, feelings, marital statuses, culture, etc. As we identify ourselves with these "things", we do not realize that we are actually masking who we truly are to the outside world, and worse, to ourselves. By masking our identities with labels instead of *just being ourselves,* we are unable to enhance the person we are. We are not *just* a police officer, we are not *just* a homemaker, we are not *just* a stubborn person, we are not *just* glad. We are not any of these labels. What we are is far greater, far superior, far more important, and far more mysterious than our mind identifies. This is why we are far more powerful than we think we are. It is for this specific reasoning that we must train our minds to diminish the "this is who I am and always will be" mindset and eliminate those feelings and labels. We are not mere things, feelings, and labels—it is only what we *think* we are and we can change that with one simple thought because we have the power within us. Let us get rid of what we thought we were and start using our powerful minds to realize *who we really are or wish to become.*

Body and mind combined, we are much more powerful than we all believe. Inside each and every single one of us, we have the power to illuminate half of the United States. How or is that possible you may ask? See, our minds and bodies run off of electricity produced from the heart and brain. We are simply individual spirits that live inside of a body mass that consists of an unlimited quantity of particles/molecules affected by positive or negative electric charges. These electric charges are controlled by our mind, both consciously and subconsciously, which then controls our everyday lives by expressing itself to the outside world through our body, attracting either positive or negative particles. Each heartbeat, each movement, and each thought we have and feel is because of the positive or negative charges that subconsciously flow through our everyday life-process, determining how we approach the world within and without. It is up to us to choose how we would like to approach the day by consciously choosing a certain frequency: Do we want to think and be positive and cast a positive bright, shining light to the world or do we want to think and be negative and cast a shadow to the world? It is up to us to change our lives using a positive mindset or devalue our lives with a negative mindset. It is up to us if we want to better our surroundings and ourselves or make it worse. It is up to us if we wish to attract a happy and bountiful environment or attract a depressing and limited atmosphere. Now, I am not here to give you a science lesson on atoms nor am I a scientist but this adjustment and explanation of life is simple. You want to get down to the nitty-gritty of atoms and have a science lesson, then go spend $12,873.23 on a semester of college and read another book! I am simply sharing with you the facts that have worked for many who chose to live a better life by adjusting their mentality into a positive form, attracting a new light. So, let us make a decision and choose to live on a positive frequency and learn that we can have a big smile on our faces for no damn reason!

Remember: Think positive, act positive, and positive things will happen. Period.

Understand Positive and Negative Electric Attraction

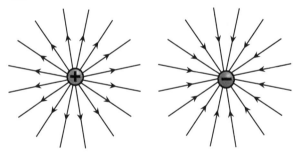

In the diagrams above, the flow of positive charges (left) and negative charges (right) can be seen. The impulse of a positive charge flows outward, which means it expands and grows, whereas the negative charge has an inward flow that decreases before stopping. Taking this into consideration, which side of the diagram do we want to be a part of? Do we want to grow and enhance our lifestyle or do we want to decrease our lifestyle? Talk about a no-brainer, obviously we wish to grow and enhance our lifestyle by being and acting positive. If you wish otherwise then close this book and go complain about life with your gang of Negative Nancies, you pansy![3]

Yes, I called you a pansy. I was negative towards you, and you may have been offended. What are you going to do about it? How are you going to take my negative comment and turn it into a positive one? Simple, you do it like this:

PMA—Positive Mental Attitude

"Whatever the mind of man can conceive and believe, it can achieve."—Napolean Hill

Positive Mental Attitude (PMA) is a philosophy that was first introduced in "Think and Grow Rich" by Napoleon Hill in 1937, which encourages one to have an optimistic view in every situation so that positive changes are attracted and achievement is increased. By having an optimistic point of view, it diverts the mind away from negativity, defeatism, and hopelessness, encouraging the mind to continually seek and execute new ways to win, find a new desirable outcome, and move forward, regardless of any circumstances.

Our mental health is an important part of our overall health because it is the main foundation in the creation of each one of us. When we are in a healthy mentality, our mind and body are more aware on how to deal with negative outcomes. If we acquire a Positive Mental Attitude, we become attracted towards developing a

3   Pansy—someone very pathetic and wimpy, generally used as an insult against both sexes.

motivated mentality, focusing on the brighter side of life, not the darker. By looking at the brighter side and having positive thoughts, other positive thoughts and actions will become attracted to us and extract the positivity that we wish to consistently be surrounded by. Likewise, staying surrounded with positive people will only help influence one another to gain a healthier and higher PMA. In doing so, we will become far more prepared for our life events by making all the necessary mental adjustments to change each negative situation into a positive one.

Techniques to Reinforce a Positive Mental Attitude (PMA)

A Positive Mental Attitude is developed by consistently reinforcing our positive thoughts, certain beliefs, new goals, shining moments, gratefulness, and good old happiness. To help guide this reinforcement we must become aware of what helps us get on a positive vibration and mood. Which tactic will help kick-start our positive frequency so we can stay motivated throughout the day or what tactic will remind us to stay inspired when we encounter a negative situation?

We will motivate ourselves through:
1. *Gratitude*
2. *Positive Affirmations*
3. *Quitting being a little bitch*
4. *Love and Forgiveness*

Gratitude

"The whole process of mental adjustment and atonement can be summed up in one word, gratitude."—Bob Proctor LIVE at SGR Seminar

Bob Proctor is right. We must acquire an attitude of gratitude! We must gratefully accept and understand all the positive and negative things that have occurred in our lives. Accept and understand that your girlfriend cheated you with "Jose the milkman who has a super thin mustache. Accept and understand that you went bankrupt from sniffing OxyContin during your lunch break. Accept and understand that you are balding from too much stress. You may ask, *"How can I accept and understand some of these things?"* Well, nobody said bettering yourself was easy, otherwise everyone would be the same. But this is why we *are different*. We accept and understand all negative and positive life situations we have encountered. This is exactly why we are the type of people that accept and understand that this is challenging. In fact, this is why it is the strongest technique to acquire in the PMA training field, because it must be practiced with consistency until it becomes habitual.

Let us adjust our minds to the reasoning that positive frequency will only attract good vibrations because when we send out good vibrations (thoughts), good vibrations will follow right back. What we put into this world, is what the world will give back. The more good vibrations that follow us back, the more good things we will receive and the more rapidly they will show up—as long as we stay in the mental attitude of gratitude. By staying on this mental frequency we are one step closer to the greater good of our goals. How do we get the ball rolling?

Simple: We begin to think of the different parts in our lives that we are grateful to have. Ever since we were kids, adults always told us to "be grateful for what you have. There are others who are much less fortunate." We may or may not have listened or understood but right now is the time to appreciate those wise words we were once told. Let us be grateful for having the sense of sight that enables us to read the book we are holding. Let us be grateful for having the sense of touch that enables us to hold and feel the pages of this book. Do you see where I am getting at (pun intended)? Be grateful that we are fortunate enough to enjoy the experiences of our senses because there are people in this world that enjoy these things. But we know nothing of those feelings because we have become accustomed to the luxuries that life has given us. Be grateful for all the good and bad that has come in and out of our lives. Be grateful for the roof over our heads, the food in our stomach, the clothes on our back, the people in our lives, and just be damn happy that you are f#$%ing alive!

Personal Activity #1: There are millions upon millions of things we can all be grateful for today. Let us sit back and really think of some of the things that have made us who we are today and be grateful for them.

   Example:

   ✓ Thank you world for giving me the power to experience life.

   ✓ Thank you world for my loving family and friends.

   ✓ Thank you world for my super cool dog, Switch, that always makes me laugh.

✓ Thank you world for the delicious homemade meat-
balls that makes me happy in the tummy.

✓ Thank you world for all the people who have f@#$ed
me over for they have made me into a stronger and
smarter person.

_____

_____

_____

_____

_____

_____

_____

_____

_____

_____

_____

_____

Positive Affirmations

Positive affirmation is a self-talk method where we
stay 100% optimistic with the words that run through our
minds as well as when we speak. There can be no hesi-
tation or doubt when we make statements to exceed our
"limitations." A limitation is something we have brought
upon ourselves to hold us back from excelling. By using
positive affirmations or self-talk, we will push through the
barriers of uncertainty, fear, and "limitation" we have subconsciously set within our minds. Positive statements like

"I am happy", "Yes I can", or "I am amazing" on a consistent and daily basis will begin to alter our subconscious mentality to think in the positive.

Are you familiar with the children's novel "The Story of the Engine that Thought It Could", later known as "The Little Engine That Could?" In this story, we clearly see the self-talk method being used with the statement "I think I can." This is a very simple story that we all read as children but were too young to understand the concept. Here is a reminder:

> *In a certain railroad yard there stood an extremely heavy train that had to be drawn up an unusually heavy grade before it could reach its destination. The superintendent of the yard was not sure what it was best for him to do, so he went up to a large, strong engine and asked: "Can you pull that train over the hill?" "It is a very heavy train," responded the engine. He then went to another great engine and asked: "Can you pull that train over the hill?" "It is a very heavy grade," it replied. The superintendent was much puzzled, but he turned to still another engine that was spick and span new, and he asked it: "Can you pull that train over the hill?" "I think I can," responded the engine. So the order was circulated, and the engine was started back so that it might be coupled with the train, and as it went along the rails it kept repeating to itself: "I think I can. I think I can. I think I can." The coupling was made and the engine began its journey, and all along the level, as it rolled toward the ascent, it kept repeating to itself: "I---think---I---can. I---think--I---can. I---think---I---can." Then it reached the grade, but its voice could still be heard: "I think I*

*can. I---think---I---can. I---think---I---can." High-
er and higher it climbed, and its voice grew fainter
and its words came slower: "I---think---I---can." It
was almost to the top. "I----think" It was at the top.
"I---can." It passed over the top of the hill and began crawling down the opposite slope. "I---think--
-I---can---I---thought---I---could I---thought---I---
could. I thought I could. I thought I could. I thought
I could." And singing its triumph, it rushed on down
toward the valley.*[4]

Did you just have an "a-ha moment?" I did too the
first time I realized this! This story is so simple yet so effective. We have overlooked little concepts of life, such as this
story, because we perceived this story to be nothing but
a children's book that was meant to be left behind in our
past and not worth reading today. Wrong! The underlying
message in this story is much more powerful than any of
us ever realized and is likely why it has become one of the
most influential pieces of literature we could ever come
across, at least in my opinion. The concept of this story
is something we should all follow and believe in order to
understand the true meaning of positive affirmations.

Personal Activity #2: Write down a list of positive affirmations you will consistently repeat to yourself, and
more importantly, will believe in when you say them.
Understand that for this exercise, repetition is mandatory.

Example:

- I AM a world champion.

- I AM a multi-millionaire.

---

4   "Story of the Engine That Thought It Could"
Published April 8, 1906. New York Tribune.

- I CAN and WILL become CEO of this company.

- I AM the hotdog-eating champion of the world.

_____

_____

_____

_____

_____

_____

_____

_____

_____

_____

_____

_____

Quit Being a Little Bitch

Stop whining and stomping your feet. This will only set you back from progressing at any moment, instantly putting you in a negative mindset. Stop complaining about why a certain situation did not go your way. Quit making excuses of how it "shoulda, coulda, woulda" happened and just get over it! Quit blaming others for changing the scenario more than we wished they had. Well, you Negative Nancy, you "shoulda" zigged when you instead zagged!

We all have situations in our lives where we wish it had gone differently and all we do is complain, dwell on failure, point the finger at others, create the scenario of how we "could" have made things differently, or, my favorite, ask ourselves "Why me?!" Well guess what, YES YOU MOTHERF@#$ER! It happened to you! Get over it! Things did not pan out the way we wished because it was our fault. It is our fault for not being mentally prepared for the outcome. It is our fault that our wife cheated on us with Eduardo, the 18-year-old pool boy with the eight-pack abs. It is OUR fault! We have to learn and accept the fact of failure and adjust our mind to create a better situation. We have to rewire our minds in a positive way in order to let things go. Because 135% of the time, it was not meant to occur at that specific point in our lives. Maybe not even at all. So, put on your big boy pants, stop complaining, put down the whaaaaamburger with extra French cries and the tall glass of Whine-eken, and quit being a little bitch.

Love and Forgiveness

"It is not how much we do, but how much love we put in the doing. It is not how much we give, but how much love we put in the giving."
– Mother Teresa

The voice and feeling of love will always point us in the right direction. Forgiveness will help us find love in certain situations where we were disappointed, disgusted, and discouraged. In order to find what we love, live our life with love, or share love with others, we must first find the love within our past, present, and future experiences. We must love and forgive ourselves for anything we have negatively done to ourselves as well as those who have negatively done to us. Yes, that means forgiving them and sending them love through our minds despite what may have happened. Forgive them for whatever "bad" they may have done to us. Forgive your best friend that stole money from you to purchase OxyContin, they were obviously going through a weak time. Forgive the ex-girlfriend who banged the mailman, she was probably confused with herself. Forgive the person who smashed your car into pieces after they cut you off, they were probably drunk and I am sure many of us are guilty of drinking and driving. Now, you might be saying to yourself, "ARE YOU F@#$ING KIDDING ME?! HOW COULD I POSSIBLY FORGIVE THEM?!" No, I am not kidding you. We have to learn to forgive them so that our lives can be filled with love and not hate. I am not saying to bring them back into your life, but to simply forgive them because they have already played their part. All we can do is figure out the limits of how close or how far we should let that person next to us, if at all. We must not be spiteful and wish them a terrible life because, as said before, it is their fault/choosing of the negative scenario they found themselves in and will attract what they deserve in life. The same goes for us, we will attract what we deserve and right now, we all deserve to have love in our lives.

Personal Activity #3: Love starts with us and it will create what we would love to experience in life. List all the negative points that have occurred in your life and those that are currently happening.

Past: _____

_____

_____

_____

_____

Current: _____

_____

_____

_____

Look over the list, let us forgive the person or people that brought upon that negativity. Let us let go of those negative times, accept that they have happened or are currently happening, and change our views on them by letting go of all the feelings associated with them. Try changing them into positive feelings by thanking each situation, person, or group of people for making us stronger, smarter, and the bigger person we are today. Those people, events, and feelings of negativity only held us back from growing beyond our potential so just let them go, for they has played their roles in our lives and it is time we move on.

Remember: If we want to grow, we must let it go.

In conclusion, realize that by having one small positive thought in the morning, our entire day, but more importantly, our entire lives, can change for the better. All the cells in our bodies react to each thought we have and whatever we put our focus and attention to. If we put all of our focus, energy, and attention into being positive and optimistic, we will only expand and grow within this world because our minds are super powerful machines that control all of the functions in our bodies. What we think about, when our feelings occur, what emotions pass through, and what we wish for, are all transformed into molecules that spread within and make us feel how we feel. We are all creators of own reality so if we believe in our visualizations, we will have the ability to create all that we wish for because everything we are, everything we have, and everything that surrounds our lives is the product our own minds created. Do you think I am lying? Roll the dice and try changing your thought patterns into positive ones and watch what happens.

STACK 3

BEHAVIOR

"The way we behave is what we become"
—Coconut Heads

Have you ever stopped to wonder about all of the capabilities we possess as humans? We have the power to take another human being's life, become a drug addict, become a priest who molests children, and give another human a five-year sentence for possession of some pure china white (cocaine). For example, let us think about criminals currently serving time in jail. They chose to be a murderer, thief, drug dealer etc. because these are all the possibilities, options, and capabilities we as humans, have. Yet, if we were the said murderer, thief, or drug dealer, we are given yet again another possibility and opportunity for early release, serve half the jail time, and be accepted back into society for good behavior. We give someone who went on a giant killing spree the opportunity to once again rejoin the community because he/she behaved while in jail. Only in America is this logical! Think about it: They behaved properly while in jail. What else are you going to do in a 4x4 square cell?! Sit back and take this mini example into perspective for a minute. Kind of blows your mind huh? Basically, we are put in a time-out in the corner and if we are on our best behavior, the punishment becomes shorter and easier. This one change in action set off a new habitual tactic of behavior that changed the course of life. Do you see the big picture here? In our world, no matter what good or bad we have done, how we have treated others or ourselves, or how we have behaved in the past, all of those actions can be altered by changing our behavior. If those who commit murder are granted a smaller punishment simply because of good behavior, then what is stopping us from doing the same and changing our behavior to produce a positive living? The answer: We are not aware of how we behave and more importantly, how to change our behavior for the better.

Creatures of Habit

Depending on the type of habits, impulses, and patterns we have, we can classify ourselves as a normal creature, an animal, or a monster. Those habits or actions that we consistently do or randomly do are what will pinpoint our true "title." For example, if you murder and decapitate your baby and shove its head in the freezer, then you would be considered a monster (true story). As living creatures, our habitual actions are highly similar to each other in a sense that we all have organs, a skeletal bone structure, a heart that pumps blood through our flesh, and a brain that sends electric currents through our bodies that causes our subconscious actions to act or react. If we become hungry, we eat. If we become thirsty, we drink. If we become horny, we hump the nearest thing around us, even if it is between the couch cushions (do not act as if you have never tried it before). These are all basic activities that our bodies will automatically do when it feels compelled to fulfill a need or desire. Accordingly, as we grow and have outer-body experiences, our minds and bodies will consciously begin to encounter different feelings of fulfillment and will seek to experience the same feelings subconsciously. In other words, if you shoot heroin and let it run through your veins, it's over Johnny! Good luck on changing that habit.

A habit[5] is an acquired mode of behavior that has become nearly or completely involuntary. It is because of these habits that the life we currently live has become, for the most part, monotonous. Let us walk through the "Average Joe's"[6] daily habitual routine. First, he will wake up, probably sometime after noon, yawn, and stretch a few times before proceeding to repeatedly scratch his genitals even though they are not itchy. His next move will then be to spark up the leftover roach (marijuana) from last night and lay in bed for another hour to scroll back and forth between Instagram and Facebook and judge every single person's post, picture and comment (awesome job, you are still in bed at one o' clock in the afternoon and you are one to judge others, makes perfect sense). Moving forward, the Average Joe will lay in bed a little longer and come up with 107 great million-dollar ideas, but act on none of them and eventually get up to shower (maybe) for his next five-hour shift that he hates going to. Friday comes and he is ready to collect his paycheck, cash it in, spend half of it on another ounce of the greenest sour diesel[7] on the block, let his girlfriend smoke half of his stash, bang her, and then ask her for some money since the remainder of his paycheck lies in the emptiness of a zip-lock bag. Eat, sleep, wash, rinse, and repeat. If we ask him what he had accomplished the day before the likely response would be "I don't know . . . Nothing really." Now,

5   "Habit.7b." Merriam-Webster.com. Merriam-Webster, n.d. Web.

6   "Average Joe"—a term primarily used in North America to refer to a completely average person.

7   Sour Diesel—also known as "Sour D." A hybrid strain of cannabis.

this is just a general example to demonstrate how many of us have no recollection of what we have done the previous day because each day is lived the same and we have become zombies and slaves to our own habitual actions. The saddest part of it all, we have no idea this is what our life has turned into.

Changing Our Habits

The first step in changing our habits is to want a positive change in our lives. Sit back, concentrate, and put into perspective what your average day looks like. Narrow it down to the day, hour, minute, and second. How exactly do you get out of bed and where do you instinctively go or do? When you put your pants on, which leg goes in first? When you drive to work, are you truly taking the quickest route or the only way you know? Yes, I know you might be scratching your head trying to remember such actions and in the order they occurred, but it is completely understandable because this is a tough scenario. Want to know a secret? We cannot think of these things down to their most minor detail because they are HABITS!

Personal Activity #1: We are creatures of habit and, as said before, sometimes we have no idea we are even performing a habit until we actually realize it. Choose any day of the week and write down or use a tape recorder (or in this generation, your smartphone) to record *exactly* what you do for every moment on said day. This activity will help us step outside of ourselves and realize what type of creature we are, what daily habits we subconsciously do, and why we do them.

     Review your list and mark off which activities you believe are irrelevant and negative to your day and change those actions before they occur or simply do not do them at all. We have to be aware and catch ourselves before we engage in certain behaviors because only then will we minimize our negative actions, replace them with positive actions, and create good habits to achieve a positive lifestyle.

Personal Activity #2: Changing our behavior is only for the better of our inner and outer selves because it will make our bodies recognize the feeling of positivity and only want more. Little by little, we can teach ourselves to recognize the feeling of change, of a different, new, and exciting form of life. Create a list of daily behaviors you will change to break your creature of habit for the better. It does not matter what it is, as long as you change!

Example:

- I will make my bed as my first accomplishment of the day.

- I will insert my left leg instead of my right leg when I put my pants on just because.

- I will start my day with a 10 minute walk to get fresh oxygen and my blood flowing.

_____

_____

_____

_____

_____

_____

_____

_____

_____

_____

_____

Bad Doggy

Breaking habits is extremely tough for anyone to accomplish, especially when you have dug yourself in a hole deeper than Aurora Jolie's rectum (Google her and thank me later). When I was 13-years-old, I dug myself into a terrible habit where I had zero idea of how much it was negatively affecting me. The habits I had picked up were not only harmful to me, but were also harmful to the people I loved. My behavior was completely erratic and unacceptable, yet I found myself this way repeatedly. I truly did not gave a f#$k about anyone, anything, and more importantly, myself. What was this terrible habit? You guessed it, it was the worst gateway drug known to man, the king of the jungle, "the Colossus of Clouts"[8] . . . alcohol.

Fun fact:

- According to the Centers for Disease Control and Prevention, "There are approximately 88,000 deaths attributable to excessive alcohol use each year in the United States. This makes excessive alcohol use the third leading lifestyle-related cause of death for the nation. Excessive alcohol use is responsible for 2.5 million years of potential life lost (YPLL) annually, or an average of about 30 years of potential life lost for each death."[9]

- Excessive alcohol consumption has become the leading cause of premature mortality in the U.S.[10]

- Excessive alcohol consumption costs the United States $223.5 billion a year with binge drinking

8   Colossus of Clouts—One of Babe Ruth's various nicknames.

9   Centers for Disease Control and Prevention. Fact Sheet-Alcohol Use and Your Health. Web. <www.cdc.gov>

being responsible for over 70% of the total costs or approximately $171 billion annually.[11]

- In 2006, there were over 1.2 million emergency room visits and 2.7 million physician office visits due to excessive drinking.[12]

These facts are pretty crazy, huh? Picture these statistics in your head the next time you decide to get behind the wheel after an all-night drinking bender. Anyway, alcohol had pretty much stolen my soul. This sinister snake had me by the neck, injecting its poisons into my jugular every single second of my life during this time. It would control my thoughts, actions, and everyday living. The problem, as if being an alcoholic wasn't enough, I would never get hangovers. Although I began to require a certain amount just to function, I never believed I had a problem. Every morning I would down a fifth of vodka right before work and drink again during work to remain stable. I even still managed to go to the gym. What did I do after the gym? Correct again! I would drink immediately after to "relax." I could honestly say I was under the influence 24/7. All of my money would be geared towards purchasing alcohol, gambling, and dating hookers. I was living the rock star life without being a rock star. When the weekend came, not only would I do my usual drinking, but I would also throw some drugs in the mix (Sorry Pete, Mom, and Dad). Luckily, I never fell too deep into drugs because I only experimented and found myself to be more of a drinker (although sometimes I wish I did drugs because alcohol became much worse). You see, the

10, 11,12   Centers for Disease Control and Prevention. Fact Sheet-Alcohol Use and Your Health. Web. <www.cdc.gov>

first bad habit led me to create a new bad one and only led me to other bad habits and harmful actions that I would normally never participate in.

Terrible things happened while I was under the influence of alcohol, but nothing really happened when I did drugs or more than likely, I was probably too drunk to realize. I allowed my life to enter a downward spiral and began living my life in ferocious gluttony. I have totaled cars, stabbed people with sharp objects, broken people's skulls open with my teeth (not exaggerating), destroyed property, and suffocated hookers (just kidding!) The list of all the terrible and harmful things I did when I was intoxicated could go on and on. I more than likely could have killed someone if I kept going down that path, but most importantly, I was killing my family, loved ones, and myself. Finally, one day I had an epiphany. My uncle died from a liver disease caused from excessive alcohol consumption and quite frankly, that wasn't the clincher. I really didn't give a sh!t when I first found out. I was dreading having to go to the funeral because I felt like I was missing out on valuable drinking time. I went, saw him lying in the casket, and simply shrugged my shoulders because I still didn't care that he was dead and was counting down the minutes until I could go into my trunk to down some Majorska. As you can see, my drinking habits led me to display disrespectful behavior towards my family and I had no idea I was acting that way because it was my subconscious reaction. The moment that changed everything was when I saw my dad looking helpless with an empty look in his eyes as if someone had sucked his soul right out of his body. His helpless stare as he stood there by the casket made my heart explode, sucked all the oxygen out of my body, and made my eyes fill up with water faster than an infant pissing in his diaper. To see my dad in such pain was, and is to this day, one of the hardest things I have ever experienced. Maybe there are worse experiences that others may have suffered, but this was the life-awakening experience that changed me forever. It was a bittersweet moment but ultimately, it took death to make me realize I needed to change my *life*.

Ok, no one gives a crap about my boo-hoo story so let's put this into a bigger perspective. Habits often cause us to spend a lot of money in the wrong places, at the wrong time, and to do the wrong thing. We'll use my alcohol habit as a number crunching example:

- (1) 5th of Majorska Vodka = $5.75 (price) x 7 (days of the week) = $40.25.

- An average night at the bar = $150.00 (money spent) x 4 (days a week) = $600.00.

- Food after the bar: Example: Pizza burger deluxe with extra disco fries = $20.00 x 4 = $80.00.

- Weekly Total = $720.25 x 4 (weeks per month) = $2,881.00 spent per month.

- $2,881 x 12 (months in a year) = $34,572.00 spent each year.

My habit cost me $34,572.00 a year! Do you realize that that is more money spent than a schoolteacher's annual salary?! Talk about bad behavior. I wasn't too worried about my alcohol consumption at all, the bigger picture was how much I was spending on consuming alcohol. Think about what we could do with that $34,572.00, and this was only from purchasing alcohol and food. We could have a brand new car, put a giant down payment on a house, open up a small business or chain of businesses, invested in kilos of gold, or purchase an overwhelming amount of "mollies"[13] to sell at the Electric Daisy Carnival. After I realized the financial burden this habit was costing me, I made some minor adjustments in my life and noticed a huge jump in my bank account. In short, cutting down on unnecessary habits will enhance your financial behavior and enhance your savings into digits you previously couldn't even count to.

Remember: "Entrepreneurship is living a few years of your life like most people won't, so that you can spend the rest of your life the way most people can't." —Unknown

Personal Activity #3: It is time to change those little habits that have altered our behavior. Part of that is changing our financial habits. Ultimately, if we rearrange the foundation of which our behavior is derived, our lives and finances will change automatically for the better. If they do not, then we must dig deeper than our financials and see what the real problem is. So, what are you spending a lot of money on? Do you own a closet full of Nikes that you have never put on? Do you have a closet filled with clothes you purchased "on sale" and never wore? How many times a week do you go out to eat? Do you really need all those Louboutins?

List all the items or habits you have or do excessively and break down how much you spend on them annually using the formula from the example above. Once you have generated a yearly sum, do your best to minimize or completely cut off these expenses.

Remember: There is no need for such materialism, especially if you cannot afford it.

---

13   Mollies—the U.S term for the drug MDMA or ecstasy

_____

_____

_____

_____

_____

_____

_____

_____

_____

_____

_____

Review your list, analyze it, and accept that changing the foundation within ourselves into a positive action is only for the better. We are literally reprogramming our brains to approach life in a brighter way, having our minds travel into a new dimension, becoming excited about our new life and new tactics.

Remember: Changing our habits changes our behavior, which in turn, changes our lives.

DREAM A LITTLE DREAM

What do we want from this world? What is it that we envision doing in this life? Many of us ask these questions from time to time, only to find ourselves thinking too much or doing too little, letting our dreams diminish because of the doubt, opinions, and distractions our environment produces. All we have are the dreams we think about, the dreams where we find ourselves doing what we love every day, enjoying the journey and being in a consistent state of euphoria. Unfortunately, the world likes to burst that dream bubble and many of us decide to tell ourselves *"It's only a dream, it's not going to come true, I should stop."* Wrong. The day you stop dreaming is the day you die inside. Our dreams do not have to be about having an abundance of money, not that any of us would mind it, but the truth is, money will make our dreams a reality. Money holds the combination to unlocking our dreams where we can live a life full of activities, where money is no object to our happiness and peace. However, in order to reach this level of freedom and happiness, we must first financially earn it. The real question is, once we are financially ready, whose and what dream are we going to fulfill? Do we dream to expand our own creativity? Do we dream to become more intuitive? Do we dream to possess new materialistic objects? Do we dream to build a family? Do we dream to travel the world? Ask yourself, are you going to live your dream or someone else's?

The American Dream

Again, many of us have no idea exactly what it is we want for ourselves. For the most part, we find ourselves wishing we could have more or have the courage to do something else, daydreaming what we could be. In reality, we are growing in a world where we are encouraged with dreams but smothered in limitations. Unknowingly, we have transformed into programmed human beings made to follow a system "the world" has created to make people financially comfortable. Our programmed brain has put a limit on our creativity and flooded our minds with fear because our minds are hypnotized by the bubble gum TV sitcoms that live happily ever after. The "happily ever after" being a great education followed by a great degree from a great college, finding a great 9 to 5 job, and living in a beautiful home with a white picket fence. This is all best described as the American Dream.

The American Dream is the vision we all have embedded in our minds that defines success. The world has made us believe we need lavish possessions and property to complete the dream. What we really do not see is that the educational system (Grades K-12) is where the brainwashing all begins. On that very first day of school, a one-way path towards College Road was unknowingly paved for us, with no detour in sight.

The education system is like an opt-in box. We often see an opt-in box when we subscribe, commonly through an inputted email address, to receive messages, news, or alerts from a specific website. We willingly enter school, some of us at preschool, others at kindergarten, with a heart and mind filled of excitement for all the marvelous messages and lessons we are going to learn. We learn from the start as kids that attending school is very important because it is there that we will acquire the tools needed to better our present and future. As so, for the next twelve years we become excited, or at least a little intrigued, about the knowledge we will acquire the following year, how we will apply it to our present and future, and how the lessons learned will only get better as we continue on through college. [Loud buzzer sound] Wait a second, can anyone explain why, in those twelve years of education, we were not provided with the message and news that we could unsubscribe/opt-out of continuing our education at college? The answer: Nobody wanted to read you the fine print at the end of the email detailing that receiving these messages was only *optional*. The system made us believe that we *needed* an education in order to have a successful life, a successful career, and any other successes we desired. Correction, any successes the system and America created for our minds to believe. Nobody wanted to tell us that it is possible to have a successful life, a successful career, and many more success without attending college. Nobody wanted to tell us that it is possible to build a life, a career, and define our own success with the help and creation of our own minds.

Now, by no means am I attempting to say college is unnecessary because I understand that there are certain occupations where an extended education is mandatory (e.g. doctors, surgeons, and lawyers). The bigger picture here is that we are led to believe that we *need* to attend college because it is the *only* way to get a great job. Is it? Is getting ass raped with a high APR for a student loan the only way to find a successful job? And when we finally do get the "dream job", is all that debt we put ourselves into to get to college worth it? The first twelve years of school was free, why charge for education after?

Let us use the beginning average New Jersey teacher salary as an example, which, according to the National Education Association, is statistically the highest paid teacher in the United States. A NJ teacher salary begins at $44, 872 and equates to approximately $33,654 after taxes. Three years and one day later, a teacher wipes the nervous sweat off their forehead, achieves tenure, and will now make a whopping annual salary of $63,111; but not before the government cuts a hole in the back pocket and that teacher is now walking away with $47,333. To put it bluntly, you probably could have earned more selling $40 bags of coke at the Jersey Shore for a summer . . . that is if you did not sniff any yourself. Now, with that annual teacher salary, we decide to follow the next step in pursuing the American Dream and we put a down payment on a $250,000 house. Consequently, we now are in debt for the next forty years between the student loan and mortgage payments. But wait! It is ok that we put ourselves in that debt because along with the great job we have, we are also able to pay into a pension/retirement plan. Interesting, so by the time we are 176,000 years old, we will *finally* have money to spend at our choosing and boy, are there countless options what we can spend it on. Should we spend it on the slot machines first, the daily pack of cigarettes, on our grandchildren, or maybe give the in-house nurse a bonus because we are too old to move around on our own at 176,000 years old? Wow, what a life we lived! The truth is, we have worked our entire lives to simply pay back the government the money they loaned us, plus interest, because we were "encouraged" to take advantage of the policies implemented by the government to pursue "our dream." Once the smoke clears, we realize that we are living beyond our means since we were pursuing a false dream. None of that money was ever ours, and neither was the dream. Society has *robbed,* yes, robbed us and our children from being able to dream on our own and use our creativity because we have been molded to surrender under someone else's control with someone else's thoughts and nothing derived from *our* own minds.

Just how brainwashed are we? If we had done our research from the beginning, before we let the world input their thoughts and dreams into our brain and making us believe they are ours, we could have discovered the following:

o   The American Dream[14] is rooted from the United States Declaration of Independence which states all men are created equal" and are "endowed by their creator with certain unalienable rights, that among are Life, Liberty, and pursuit of Happiness."

o   In "The Epic of America", written by James Truslow Adams in 1931, the idea of the American Dream was described as "life should be better and richer and fuller for everyone, with opportunity for each according to ability or achievement."[15]

o   There is NO true definition for the American dream.

The Declaration of Independence states we are all free to live, free to be free, and free to pursue our happiness. So if we are free to be free and free to pursue our

---

14   "The American Dream"—Web.Wikipedia, the free encyclopedia. <www.wikipedia.com>

15   "James Truslow Adams"—Web. Wikipedia, the free encyclopedia. <www.wikipedia.com>

happiness, why is it that we are not free to decide if college and the "American Dream" is the right choice for us? Why is it wrong to dream if we are by law given the right to life and liberty? The answer is right in front of us: The world has taken it upon itself to tell us how and when it is okay to dream and when it is or is not ok to be free. Need proof? When James Truslow Adams published his book, he was convinced by others not to keep his original book title "The American Dream" because the world was presently fighting the Great Depression and the dream was in danger. Why did he have to change his book title? Who felt entitled to deprive him, the author, to name his own book the way he wanted to? When John Lennon was five years old, his mother (allegedly) always told him *happiness is the key to life.* When he went to school and was asked what he wanted to be when he grew up, he wrote down "happy." They told him he didn't understand the assignment, and he in return told them they did not understand life.

Remember: *Those that live the American Dream are those who cannot dream for themselves.*

The American Lie

The world has brainwashed us all into not thinking for ourselves and only the intelligent can see this view. Did you know that 97% of the people in this world are working for the other 3% and 3% of the people in this world are earning 97% of the money? This is a F%$@ KING fact and if you do not believe me, then "Google" it. I double-dog dare you.

If we were to step outside our bodies for a second and dig into our souls, we would find out that most of actually *do* know what we want. The problem is we have no idea how to get what we want and have therefore convinced ourselves that it is impossible to achieve. We have convinced ourselves it is impossible to reach a financial status that nearly everyone dreams of because we have been brainwashed to believe that we do not deserve to be part of the elite. Says who?! We have convinced ourselves that it is wrong to daydream because it was wrong to do so in the classroom when we were meant to be paying attention. Again, says who?! This has all happened because we have been brainwashed to believe that the structure of the school system is the only way to make it in this world. However, what the school system failed to teach us is how to *earn* money, how to be *creative,* and how to just be who we want to be. For example, time was wasted on teaching us bullshit stories on world history, only to find out a few decades later that it was all a good movie plot.

Here is a good "movie plot": Thanksgiving. Thanksgiving is a day we all cherish, as we unite to remind ourselves the meaning of family and friends, and give thanks for our many blessings. We do just as the Pilgrims and Indians did on that special day when they both united to share a meal together and agree that both groups were equal and both could live happily together. [Loud buzzer sound] Wait a minute, did everybody forget that the Pilgrims actually barged into the Indian's land, set it on flames, robbed them for all they had, killed an astronomical amount of people, raped their women, and took over the land that we now call America? We do not realize that what actually happened was the Pilgrims offered a turkey to the remaining Indians as a peace offering for having killed their entire tribe and ruining their land. Talk about an even trade! I mean, don't get me wrong, I am very grateful for Christopher Columbus discovering this land, otherwise many of us would not be living here, but why all the fluff? How much fluff are the history books going to feed us? Just tell the real story! We might as well throw in the Tooth Fairy and the Chupacabra in the history books; it makes for a nice story. On the contrary, we cannot blame and pass judgment on the creators for wanting to make money. Instead, we must blame ourselves for being naïve enough to believe in their stories

This system is not about education, this system is based on grades, on how much information one can consume and memorize. News flash: No amount of reading or memorizing will make us successful in life. It is the understanding and application of wise thought that counts (thank you, Bob Proctor).The system has failed to show us how to apply our knowledge to real life and only taught us how to apply it on paper and how to compete against other students for the best grades. Subsequently, it has become instinctive for us to be in a competitive mindset and out of the creative mind. Without the creative mind, nothing in this world would be here because everything we currently have or see started as a simple, creative thought. If Thomas Edison did not daydream or have the creative mind to invent the light bulb then we would all still be reading under a candle. If Alexander Bell did not daydream or have the creative mind to invent the telephone then we would all still be contacting one another through a telegraph. To have our creative minds limited because of some demonic system that this world created is nothing but f!@#ing bullspit! At least in my book.

Personal Activity #1: Everyone in this world has their own personal preference as to what they want out of life and what makes them happy. However, do you not want more? What is it that you catch yourself daydreaming about when you step into your subconscious? What the

F#$K is it that you want?! Bet you $500 that your answer is financial freedom. Thought so—pay up!

List all the things you would do or the items you would purchase if you had financial freedom.

_____

_____

_____

_____

_____

_____

_____

_____

_____

Look at your list and focus on how it would make you feel if you had such items or could do such actions. Repeat this list to yourself every-f@#$ing-day with positive affirmation. By consistently reminding ourselves what we want in our lives and using repetition, we will attain all that we seek.

A Catholic Cash Connection

I want to share with you all a dream I personally witnessed in my life and illustrate how money is truly the key to unlocking any dream we have.

My parents were born and raised Roman Catholics from the Philippine Islands. My grandparents were Catholics, my aunts and uncles are Catholic, my cousins are Catholic, my brother Pete was a Catholic, and his "fawthor" was a mechanic (Marisa Tomei My Cousin Vinny reference: Had to do it!). Hopefully you are somewhat understanding just how Catholic my family was. To my parent's dismay, Pete and I were not the angelic children they hoped for and we were considered what most Catholics might define as "sinners." We were constantly in and out of confession and forced to say a thousand and one "Our Father's" and "Hail Mary's" to beg for forgiveness like a bad bog that just took a sh@t all over the new white carpet. By the time I was in the third grade, my brother and I were both kicked out of Confraternity of Christian Doctrine (CCD) school and the only light at the end of the tunnel was that both he and I had completed our communion just like my parents had hoped for. Again, to my parent's dismay, we were never able to complete our eighth grade confirmation because we were not allowed back in Catholic school. Five years later, we take a family vacation to the Philippine Islands and my parents thought it would be a great idea for my brother and I to complete our Catholic journey and have our confirmations there. The reasoning behind this decision was because they wanted to fulfill their dream of raising good and respectful Catholic children. Now for those that may not be aware, in order to make your confirmation you must complete eight years of CCD education; something my brother and I obviously failed to accomplish. So how would we be able to make our confirmation? Cha-ching! You guessed it, money. At the age of 13, dressed in a translucent uniform and sweating more than a fat kid trying to tie his sneaker, I witnessed firsthand how my mother handed the priest a stack of U.S dollars bigger than the Wall Street Journal to fulfill her dream. After the transaction, the priest slapped on his neck strap, pasted the sign of the cross on my forehead with Blistex, and muffled under his breath a small prayer to shoo away the sparks of Lucifer inside of me. Now, is this priest truly part of a prophecy or is he really a profit-seer? My brother and I were old enough to understand what was taking place and it was at that specific moment that we learned what money does. No matter where we want to go, what we want to achieve, or what the dream consists of, money will get you there and people will do whatever it takes to fulfill that dream. I learned that money is the bridge we must use to fulfill our dream of success. Looks like WWE superstar The Million Dollar Man was right: "Everybody has a price."

The experience of "successfully completing my confirmation" opened my eyes to a different light and I developed a "Holier-Than-Thou" attitude. Immediately, I realized that this Catholic religion system was a joke to us all, was manipulated by money, and the "heads-in-chair" were nothing but fugazis[16]. If they could act self-righteous, give the cold shoulder, and display moral superiority to those whose beliefs or actions do not follow theirs, then why should I not do the same? I would steal clothes from the mall and sell them for a discounted price. I would fill up small zip-lock bags with oregano, spray some Cool Water cologne in them, and sell it to kids as the "sweetest weed" on the block. I would steal car parts and sell them out of my parent's garage. As you can see, I became quite the hustler but I looked at this way: If the priest could

16   Fugazi—a slang term for people or items that are artificial, fake, or false.

accept "donations" for breaking the rules, why the f%$k couldn't I do the same? You see, we need to accept that we occasionally have to break the "rules" to get what we want. If we want to live a life with ample freedom, then we must take action to earn the money to do so. I am not saying to break the law and put yourselves at risk for ten years in jail, but do something differently than others and different than what you are comfortable doing. There will be people who disagree with your actions and there will be times when you become unsure if you are doing "the right thing." FOGETABOUT IT (Did you mean: *forget about it*). That sh@t does not matter. The only thing that matters is your dream. Whatever or whomever stands in the way of you accomplishing your dream is not meant to be part of your journey. Unbelievably, those who tend to disagree with our actions are the ones who are jealous. Jealous because we are doing what they only wish they could. To those people and the Jiminy Cricket in our minds that tells us what "the right thing" to do is or that we are not capable of doing something, we have to say, "GO F@$K YOURSELF!" Why? Because they are the ones who do not understand that earning enough money is the only way to achieve the life we dream of having and that is ok because everyone has different dreams, opinions, and perspectives. Let others think how they would like just as we will do the same, except we will not judge others' preferences.

Personal Activity #2: We all sit and dream about how we wish we could travel or save all of the starving children around the world. How can we do that? Money. Money will help us pursue the dream that has been sitting in our stomachs for years. Let us untie that knot in our belly, step out of our comfort zone, and start taking risks. It is these

risks, specifically financial risks, that will open new opportunities. Our first call to action is to figure out how
to earn our dream. That is right, earn it and do whatever
the f#$k it takes to get us on that first class ticket to our
dream.

List three risky things you are going to do differently to earn money and get you one step closer to achieving a dream.

1. _____

_____

_____

2. _____

_____

_____

3. _____

_____

_____

Enough of the pity-party, let us start believing in
our dreams and seek that
missing piece of the puzzle
we all search for: Happiness.
We must live our lives in fulfillment in order to feel the
complete happiness we each
deserve in our lives. We all
deserve nothing but the great-
est and to enjoy each amazing

and exciting moment through our own eyes, the way we wish to live it and not the way others tell us. Time for us to *live our dreams.* So kids, the next time your teacher says "Hey! Stop daydreaming and pay attention", tell them to go eat a d@#. You are paying attention: Attention to what you want.

STACK 5
SURROUNDINGS

Open Up and Absorb Your Positive Surrounding Like a Chameleon

Be aware of your surroundings. We all have certain goals we wish to accomplish yet the majority of us have no idea where to start and/or become discouraged along the journey. We have set a list of goals, ready to go after them full throttle with the intention of accomplishment, and all by ourselves, because we believe whole-heartedly that we can handle such situations. Day in and day out, we soon realize how tired, discouraged, and pissed the f@#k off we are getting at ourselves for not being able to accomplish certain parts of our journey. Now we find ourselves swimming in mud and before we know it, we are drowning in our feces from all the sh!t we have put ourselves through. Naturally, we begin to ask ourselves, *why did this happen, how did this happen, and what went wrong.* Easy, we did not place ourselves in the correct atmosphere. By not seeking help, we actually put ourselves in a situation further away from our goals only to aimlessly be walking in circles more confused than a foreign exchange student trying to find the cafeteria who ended up in the boiler room licking a melted, lint-filled Hershey's kiss from his pocket as lunch.

So now let us think, how come the foreign exchange student ended up in the boiler room instead of having himself a nice lunch in the cafeteria? Simple, he should have asked for help! Remember people, we are only human. We often convince ourselves that we can do things on our own and that asking for help is for the weak. WRONG! Sometimes, we cannot do things on our own, especially if we have no idea about the subject of our goal. Every professional, every successful person, basically everyone in general, needs help to get where they are looking to go. We need guidance. Look at it this way: When we need to travel to an unknown location, we instantly seek directions. We are not going to get there unless we ask the GPS, Google Maps, or even pull over to a gas station and asking for directions from someone who is familiar with the area. Because we are driving to an unfamiliar place, are we just going to hop in the car and say "Eehhh let's see what happens." No! We are going to end up more confused than a fat kid at a Whole Foods; meaning we will have no idea where we are or what to do.

The goal we have set is for our best interest therefore, it is in our best interest to find someone who is a professional in the area of our goal. Those professionals will provide us with the directions to that final destination that is unknown to us but familiar to them. For example, if your goal were to open an ice cream parlor, you would begin by contacting someone who owns a chain of TC-BY's. If they do not respond, then contact someone who owns a chain of Carvel locations. The confronting task is to get in contact with someone who has already been through the process and is willing to help others who wish to follow in those footsteps. More importantly, it is better that you try to communicate with successful people and get your message out there because you never know what will pop out.

Remember: *"When it comes to creativity, there is no competition. The goal is that we both make it."*
—Unknown

Wipe Your Ass and Clean Out the Crap

We have now successfully selected our destination and have acquired the directions to get there but now we ask ourselves, "How can I get there faster?" Better yet, the correct question is "How can I get there *correctly* and in a more *beneficial way*".

Do you remember that phrase we often heard as kids and teenagers "Be careful, those kids are not a good influence on you?" Well, unbelievably, this has to be asked once again and applied to our current life. If we are trying to achieve our goal, with our best interest in mind, it would not be wise to hang out with degenerates, losers, or any other kinds of people that will bring us and our morale down. No matter what the relationship is, take a step back, look from the outside in, look inside each individual, and ask yourself *"Is this person a negative influence on me?"* You have to question everyone from your best friends, siblings, teammates, girlfriend, boyfriend, coworkers, the mailman, neighbor etc. Are they happy or are they just living day to day with a "woe is me" attitude? Are they acting on the present to help their future? Or are they dwelling on the past like a 40-year old man at a bar telling everyone how great of a quarterback he was in high-school as he is yelling at the football team on TV on what plays they should be running? Well, if he knew so much and was *that* great of a quarterback then why isn't he on the field? Because, this 40-year old man is a has-been who is trying to arm wrestle everyone at the bar to prove "he's still got it" and is living in the past. We all know and have seen these types of people and most likely have a few of them hanging around us. You have to ask yourself, *are they doing better today than they were last year, or are they still stuck and bitter?* In all seriousness, take a step back and look at the people that surround your life. Now take their life into perspective and see how, and if it does, <u>help</u> you become closer to your goals. Nine times out of ten, that individual is holding you back.

Many of us may not realize it but we spend so much time, I mean SO much time, keeping people around that don't belong and more than likely, it is an individual portraying a negative influence without us even realizing it is happening. If time was not enough, we are also spending innumerous amounts of energy towards keeping that individual company and listening to his or her "complaints" and trying to comfort them by saying, "everything is going to be okay." Well you know what? Everything is NOT going to be okay because it is not okay that we are wasting time and energy on someone who is just bringing us mentally and physically down. Negativity will sucker punch us, leave us on the ground, and kick us again while we are down. These negative people, and only you know who those are, do not want to better themselves, they just want someone to wallow with them in their pity as they are smoking their 13th cigarette of the day and "swearing" they are going to start bettering themselves by smoking this last one. Unfortunate as it may be, 99.9% of the time, the person closest to us is the one who is holding us back from becoming the best person we can be. We need to eliminate these negative people from our lives and surround ourselves with positive people who look at life in a much brighter light. No matter how close the relationship is, we have to get rid of them. The act of getting rid of negative people will either turn our stomach for the better or for the worse. Better because we can finally remove the individual or group that we have struggled to get rid of and haven't had an opportunity to do so or worse, because we are not ready for what we are about to do. Overall, it is time to tell those negative people to F$%K OFF and take a hike!

Personal Activity #1: As painful as it may be, be honest and list three people or items you feel are currently negative in your life.

1. _____
   _____

2. _____
   _____

3. _____
   _____

Now find yourself a bright red marker and draw a giant 'X' through that entire list. Cross them out of your life, literally, and make a decision for yourself that you will no longer affiliate with these negative people. Cut the umbilical cords and realize that it is time for you to grow the f$%k up and grow some balls, aka confidence!

Remember: *The truth is, people want to see you do well in life, but never better than them.*

Escape Your Comfort Zone

Everything currently surrounding us provides us with some form of comfort, hence we create our comfort zone and do not become aware of our surroundings because we are trapped in monotony. The comfort zone is, in my opinion, a fatal and extremely deadly place to be for someone who is striving to better his or her lifestyle. Many of us, including myself at one point, are likely to be stuck inside a rhythm of mediocrity. For example, we wake up, smack on our best smile, and get to work with a group of co-workers who high-five each other after every sale as the manager cheers everyone on. Meanwhile, we are making a mediocre salary by being paid an hourly rate with no incentives. By the time Friday rolls around, we are ready to loosen our collars and spend half of our paycheck on Miller Lights and disco fries at 3am, but what and why are we celebrating? In reality, we just spent over 40 hours working on accomplishments that are set by someone else who makes everyone else think it is their own. Paints an entirely different picture doesn't it? It is understandable that we are not seeing these things because our vision is obscured with the image of stability we have created in our lifestyle and the people we work with.

Stability is the key element everyone on this planet tries so hard to find and once that day comes, we stick with it because we know it will never fail. The stable job is earning you *just enough* to live your current lifestyle, pay the mortgage or rent, go out occasionally to a nice restaurant, drive around in a brand new leased car; you know the basics. Now, I am not trying to disrespect anyone because I truly believe everyone has his or her own preference of lifestyle as well as level of success and if that is fine with you than it is fine with me and you should probably put this book down because you are obviously happy. However, do you sometimes have that feeling that you deserve more for yourself? Well guess what, YOU DO! The reason you are not accepting that you deserve more for yourself is because most of the time you have been taught to think like everyone else and have not given yourself the opportunity to challenge yourself and expand your mind. We are too scared to do something extra that is outside of the box and outside of our comfort zone. We have so much more inside of us and if we stay in our comfort zone and stay around the people who 'comfort' us by giving us the "Hey, at least you tried" bullshit, we are not helping ourselves in bringing out our maximum potential. Those who give us the "hey, at least you tried" talk are not the ones we need in our lives, we need people that are positive and will challenge our mind and body. We need positive people that will tell us "yep, you did that wrong, but here may be a way to fix it" or "you could have done better." These positive people that do not give us the pat on the back with the "at least you tried" assurance enable us to create mini challenges inside our lives or in our workplace and work together. We need to build a good team of sparring partners to help one another get better and better through every challenge. Step out of that comfort zone for crying aloud! Be spontaneous and put down that $500 on 23 red at the roulette table occasionally! We all know that every single time you have approached the table you've seen someone else do it and wished you had the guts to do it, too. Well, do it! Do something outside of your comfort zone. You never know, you just might walk out a winner, but if you lose, "hey, at least you tried", right?

Personal Activity #2: Be honest and list three items small or big that are challenging to you. After you write them down, choose different days to face each challenge. It is always good to do something challenging or different in your life because that is the only way you will expand your mind and see the world in a new perspective. The bigger your world, the bigger your perspective and the better your surroundings will become.

1. _____

2. _____

3. _____

Get Off Your Ass and You Find that F@#King Dog

 Now that we have successfully walked outside of our comfort zone and left our security blanket at home, it is time to do the footwork. It is now time to get out there, begin the research towards our goals, and find the professionals. It is now time to find that world champion that has made millions of dollars in the specific industry/business we are in or trying to reach and ask him or her to show us the ropes. Look for the masterminds of successful people and ask to join; just open your damn mouth and contact anyone who is a success! Be relentless and annoying until you are satisfied with the response you are seeking. However, if that is not

the approach for you, then simply surround yourself with positive people even if they have nothing to do with your goals, because this overall positivity is going to uplift your spirit. Now that all of our cookies are in one jar, set up meetings with them and pick at their brains so you can understand how his or her idea came about, how it worked, and how it made him or her successful today. Trust when I say this, *placing yourself in the correct atmosphere and surroundings is only going to help you get better and closer to your goals.* You will learn what the hard and easy times were, what price to pay and the price to stay, and most importantly, what helped get him or her into the successful position they are currently in. Would it not be much easier for us to find out how this world champion created their success and just so happens to be the goal you are wishing to achieve? The answer is a thousand times YES! We *want* to talk with these people and feed our open mind with the powerful knowledge being given so that, once again, we can take a step back and put all of this into perspective and see how we need to adjust it to suit our goals, our success, and our lives.

Personal Activity #3: List three different people who are currently successful, whether you know them or not, with the same goals as you and list the ways you will try to contact them.

1. _____

2. _____

3. _____

Remember: *Be aware of your surroundings. For each person who has walked in and out of our lives has molded a piece into the creation of who we are today.*

FIGHT THE FEAR

"Anything you fight to get, you must fight to keep"
—Bob Proctor, SGR Seminar

Do you remember the very first time you fell in "love" with that special someone? How you became speechless because their beauty and presence ignited the room with such flamboyance and there were no words to describe the feeling? How with every passing second, you caught yourself daydreaming about that person and all it would do was set your heart and stomach on fire at an uncontrollable speed? How every song had a meaning and somehow your thoughts were always towards that one beautiful picture of you and that special someone? Yes, the feeling as if Hulk Hogan landed the "Big Boot" to your mid-section. Coincidentally, just as you are thinking about that person, they walk in and your thoughts change into nothing but confusion. Your stomach is imploding, your palms are sweaty, knees are weak (mom's spaghetti), and your brain is scrambled like a three-cheese omelet. You put those feelings aside and map out a plan in your head as he or she sits down in the cafeteria. The timing and setting is perfect for you to make your move, so you slowly recite to yourself the well-thought out plan you created to speak to this individual. Nothing could ruin the perfect moment that was about to happen. Suddenly, as you start to get up from your seat, ready to engage in full force like a wild gorilla escaping the zoo, you sit yourself back down. You sit back down with doubt and wonder, *"What if she says no?"* You confidently decide to yourself she will not say no so you try a little harder to get up, and once *again,* you sit back down with another excuse. *"I'm not wearing my lucky Chicago Bills three-peat t-shirt today; I'll talk to her tomorrow."* Once again, you decide it is now or never and want to give it another shot by taking a deep breath to find the confidence to get up. You take the first step away from your seat and . . . BAM! You are open handed by fear. *"Holy sh!t what am I crazy! She could never like a loser like me! She probably hates the Bulls!"* Nevertheless, you retreat to your comfort zone by sitting back down to eat the same peanut butter and jelly sandwich with the crusts cut off, watching the nervous sweat drip off your fingerprints and melt into your bread to create a fat boy finger fossil. You continue to sit there and wonder if your dream will ever come true as you bite into the soggy-sweat filled sandwich that mom made with pride, only for you to swallow each bite with sorrow.

Day in and day out, you convince yourself to forget the doubts, to forget the excuses, to forget the fear, and to find the courage to get up from your seat. To your dissatisfaction, you get the same exact outcome as the day before. Days, months, and years fly by and your dream has yet to become true, and you are still sitting in the same exact seat with your head down in frustration. Time has flown by so quickly that one day you look up and realize it is high school and you are still sitting in the same chair with the same peanut butter and jelly sandwich with the crusts cut off, and the same Chicago Bulls three-peat t-shirt you cannot take off because you are too fat. That day you look up is also the day you find out your dream girl is going to the senior prom with some varsity jacket-wearing-douchebag that is more than likely going to shove alcohol down her throat so he can pop that cherry you have been trying to sniff for half a decade. Two years later, you find out she is an oxycodone-sniffing- drug-addict because of the traumatic prom experience of 1997. As so, you wipe the sweat off your forehead and confidently tell yourself, *"Wow, I'm glad I never hooked up with that girl! Look at what happened to her!"*

Reality check: She became a drug addict because you did not have the balls to talk to her in the 6th grade. You left your dreams to shatter because you were stuck in a mirage that fear created. Who knows, maybe you could have been the deciding factor that changed her destiny for the better, but I guess you will never know. With that said, I congratulate you. I congratulate you on accomplishing nothing except having an overwhelming amount of skid marks in your Fruit-of-the-Looms. (For your information [FYI], this was my experience and my Fruit-of-the-Looms.)

Fear—1, You—0.

You see, for every second that goes by there is constant fighting going on inside of us. Some fights are so easy that we subconsciously do not even recognize there was even a fight going on in the first place. Then there are the tough fights, ones where we cannot even bear the mere thought of them because we might snap, so we decide the best solution is to retreat. Wrong, we chose the cowardly solution. What we must learn, as individuals who want to grow, is to transform the tough fights we retreat from into the easy fights we don't even notice. I know, easier said than done. We must do this because fear is the number one super villain and the kryptonite to our souls that exists in our solar system. This super villain is immortal, will never go away, will poison our minds and bodies, varies in size and power, and will hunt us down our entire lives as long as we decide to stay inferior. Our weakness gives fear the power to kill us at any speed it wishes with its ruthless actions. We can die a slow death, a fast death, or the worst kind of death—death while still alive. Fear can take our insides for keeps and leave us empty and incapable of growing. Fear is the kind of super-villain that will use its power to take away our power to love, rip it into shreds of confetti, and throw it in the air during the celebration of a new marriage. *"Do you take FEAR into holy matrimony until DEATH do you part? I do."* Yet, did you know that we also possess superpowers of our own that can be enhanced the more we search for it? That's right, we have the super-hero powers to crush fear dead in its tracks, diminish the thoughts of it, and suck the negative spirits right out of its heart. Enough is enough, let us start striking back at our fears and begin to develop the fighter that is inside all of us. So the next time we are asked to enter into matrimony again with fear, we will boldly say, *"I do not."*

How Do We Defeat Fear?

The million-dollar question is . . . how do we defeat fear? Ding! Ding! Ding! The answer is: We will defeat fear by facing it. The journey may be long and we might not necessarily achieve exactly what we first envisioned, but just by facing the fear and fighting for what we believe in is a triumph against fear in itself. Just by facing our fears, we have made the internal fight a little easier to grasp and will begin a journey of persistent progression that knocks our fears out one by one. In doing so, we will bring about a clearer vision of our goals and release the fog that our fears had originally created around them. Each fear that we face and surpass will now transform into one less we will never have to worry about again.

By facing our fears one by one, our bodies will begin to receive the message from our subconscious to turn those instincts of fear into the instincts of a fighter. By becoming a fighter, we will train our mind and body to react differently towards the feelings of nervousness that doubts, excuses, and fears have created. With a nervous stomach burning, sweaty palm dripping, scrambled-egg brain thoughts and feelings beginning to occur, our new inner body will automatically adjust itself into fight mode rather than retreating and being defeated by our inner demons, aka "The Villain."

Courage is a characteristic that lies within all of our spirits. Some of us know how to bring our courage to the surface of fear, but some of us do not. We all have something we fear, something that gives us anxiety, something that puts us at total discomfort, something that makes us want to crawl into a hole and hide. Those are the literal powers of fear where it can bring us to our extreme weakness. It is at these moments, when we feel the butterflies swarming in our stomachs like killer bees on fire that we need to act. It is at these very moments when the thoughts of being rejected, neglected, losing, and discomfort we need to strike back the most. We need to learn to take action when fear sets in, not when we feel comfortable. Because facing fear when we are at ease is not truly facing fear. Instead, we must be at the opposite and feel completely helpless and mentally shut down by the cause of fear. When this feeling of vulnerability hits, we must act immediately and let the courage sink in so we can mentally push through those thoughts and feelings of fear.

Let us finally put our fears to rest and use our newfound courage to put our best foot forward, with no doubts or worries about the outcome, and slay the inner demons. Whether we win, lose, succeed, or fail, we are stilling facing our fear instead of running away. If we can accomplish this and face our fears one by one, then we are one step closer to our goals in life, one step further away from our fear, and one step closer into growing into the courageous person we truly are.

Personal Activity #1: Everyone has something he or she wishes to accomplish, an accomplishment that has been running around in our brains like a hamster on a wheel. It is time to break that wheel and chip away at this so-called villain (fear) who is preventing us from reaching our goals.

In any order you like, list below all your fears that you believe are preventing you from accomplishing your goals and achieving success. These fears could range from approaching a person and asking them on a date to going on a rollercoaster to scratching your nails on a chalk board, or even walking through a cemetery. No matter the reasoning, a fear is still a fear.

_____

_____

_____

_____

_____

_____

_____

_____

_____

_____

_____

        Look at your list and determine which fear is the easiest and which is the hardest. Once you have decided, rank the remaining fears on the list according to lowest and highest. You have now created your scale of fear and, as a person who wishes to stand up to it, face a new one day by day. This practice will help you jump out of your comfort zone and realize that your fear really was not as bad as you thought.

Personal Activity #2: One of the many fears we all have in common is the fear of earning money, so in the words of Jim Young from Boiler Room, "Pick your skirts up, grab your balls, and let's make some fucking money!" Make a list of items you wish money could buy or an amount of money you would like to have and then answer the following:

- What is holding you back from achieving this?

- What do you fear will happen if you release the fear that is holding you back?

Example:

- Wish: I would like to earn $100,000 a year.

- Holdback: My 9am-5pm job.

- Fear: Not being able to pay my bills

- Solution: Quit my job and do not pay my bills

Wish: _____

_____

_____

Holdback: _____

_____

_____

Fear: _____

_____

_____

Solution: _____

_____

_____

This example may sound ridiculous and you are probably in disbelief, but it is really not that crazy. The fear is to be incapable of paying the bills if you quit your job. However, by quitting your job, you now have to figure out a way to pay the bills and earn $100,000—also known as fighting the fear. If you are in a place where you do not wish to be, then leave. I understand that this may sound a little dramatic and I get some circumstances are different than others, but if you still are shaking your head in disbelief than I guess this book is not for you. Have fun at your 9-5 job and the annual $0.10 raise (as the government keeps raising the taxes in America) and enjoy your life filled with fear.

Remember, even though we are growing, fear never dies. Fear will always make a comeback at different points in our lives and present itself in a new form. Each new fear will be tougher than the previous one, casting a darker shadow on us. But it doesn't mean that it cannot be beat. We will stand our ground, believe we can overcome each fear, and beam our true light through every single one. If we persistently shine our light to fade out the darkness of fear . . . then the joke is on fear itself.

STACK 7
MONEY

"For the love of money is a root of all kinds of evil. And some whose hearts were fixed on it have been turned away from the faith and been wounded with innumerous sorrows" (Timothy 6:10).

Generally, this is the moral that all the religions in the world have unanimously taught us since we were young and ever since, have tried to convince the masses that an overabundance of money will more than likely lead to a path of destruction and evil. However, in order to alter the path of evil or forgive any evil action, one should donate towards the good. The good being defined as your place of worship. Yet, is your money really turned into "good money?" Is your money now seen as good because it has been blessed by your place of worship, only to later find out that the priest, dean, father etc., is getting wasted and molesting poor little Johnny the altar boy? But hey, let's just say ten Hail Mary's followed by a few Our Father's and just like that . . . you are completely forgiven! Hopefully, this example is opening your eyes to a bigger picture. However, if you are shaking your head in disagreement let it be known that this is just my opinion and "only God can judge me", right?

Instead, let us open our mind to the philosophy that:

"There is no good money. There is no bad money. There is just money." —Charles "Lucky" Luciano

Money is an extremely powerful note. It can chew us up, spit us back out, and give us a golden shower[17] while we are laying on the ground if we let it. Money is so powerful that it can alter any decision in an instant and force the human mind to enter a dimension it never knew existed because it can enhance any part of the mind, body, and soul when we choose to magnify it. Why? Because money is, once again, so powerful that 135,653% (I am exaggerating, but not really) of the time it will control us all as human beings. We may not recognize it but money will make us its unforgiving slave, simply because it is extremely difficult for us to control.

It is possible to lose control of who we are because money is a tool that will enhance who we already are on the inside or who we wish to become. We need to understand that money should only create and/or enhance a better lifestyle and help those individuals who are important to our personal life because, as natural humans, we do not realize when money is taking us further in life or extremely further *from* it. We must learn to be careful where we use it, what we use it for, and how we distribute the money earned. Once again, we are only human and it is very easy for us to become lost in the transition when we start seeing all the zeroes lining up. But remember, we must put greed, jealously, and competitive thoughts away if we wish to achieve our financial goal. In other words, do not be a stupid d!#khead[18] because there is more than enough money in the world for everyone to share and enough money to create the lifestyle we wish to have. (We can thank the Federal Reserve for that.)

17   Golden shower—the act of urinating on another person
18   Dickhead—an extremely stupid or contemptible person

But before we can learn how to not let money control us, we first have to earn it and figure out how to manage it. And in case you live on another planet, earning money and being able to manage it correctly by placing it in the "correct" hands is not hard; it's F#$%ING HARD! The only way we can overcome this challenge is by learning to believe in ourselves and truly understand that only we know what will be the best way to earn money and believe in ourselves to take action. Believe in that great idea that has been sitting inside waiting to come out and put all of your thoughts to work with positive affirmations so you can progress. Believe in that craft you possess, no matter what it may be because everyone in this world is different and possess different skills. Some are skilled mechanics, hairstylists, or pole dancers. Some are destined to be in the casinos because they know how to gamble well and become rounders[19]. Others still, have personalities that make them a great salesperson or leaders in multi-level marketing programs, also known as pyramid platforms. No matter the case, the overall gist is that we all possess something special within us and we have to believe in our choice of earning money. Along with this decision, we must be aware that there will be people who will try to knock us down with negativity and question our actions or, my personal favorite, "it's not an honest living." You know what, GO SUCK AN EGG! Tell those people to go scratch as they live their life in content and monotony. We set ourselves apart from everyone else in this world because WE ARE HERE TO MAKE F!@#ING MONEY and step out of the average lifestyle. We are here to grow and become the best person we can be. It is for that reason that we must stand our ground with strong and positive

19   Rounders—a player who knows all the angles and earn his living at the poker table.

intentions, and not let anyone or anything get in the way of our choices and our path of making money. With that said, remember that everyone is different with his or her own preferences and beliefs; what is right for one may not be right for another.

Remember: There is no right and wrong, there is just different.

There Is No Such Thing as a Halfway Crook

Do you ever cross the street without looking both ways? No, right? Well, the same goes for our lives because we must have our eyes wider than an owl to be aware of our surroundings. All around us there are thieves, robbers, sticklers, and crack-heads that will do anything to snatch a buck. Right away, I bet you pictured a scraggly old man with soy sauce stains all over his torn-up sweater or a stick-up kid with a .45 to your chest. Wake up and smell the Dutch oven! We need to be weary of the money sharks swimming around us, not the average robber pointing a gun in your ribs at the ATM. Those who look you straight in the eyes, blind you with their sparkling smile and Lumineers, and pitch you to death about a promising future with financial freedom are the real money-hungry sharks. It is the internet sales who are "willing to share their secrets" on how we can all make $135,000 in one month or the pyramid platforms where the products are pushed down your throat, told a remarkable story of how great the company is, and promised a ton of money if you join. The fact is, most money sharks are very manipulative, relentless, ruthless, lethal, and could sell shoes to a snake or leave your pockets emptier than a fat kid's

Trick-or-Treat bag on November 1ˢᵗ. We must learn to either keep our guards up or be aware of the shark tactics. Or, better yet, become a money shark ourselves because to beat the shark, we must eat the shark.

We live in such a money-hungry world that people will take us for every single dollar and suck us dry once we hand them a cent. They are thirsty for blood money[20] and for that reason we need to become aware of just how dangerous it is to swim in a pond filled with sharks. These sharks (anyone looking to take your money) will eat you alive once you give them a taste of your own blood. It is because of them and the rest of the world that we need to keep our guards up and not let anyone pull the wool over our eyes. But what if we cannot beat them? Should we join them instead? That decision is based upon preference and what we are willing to do to achieve our dream. Only by being on full alert with our mind, body, and soul will we know who and what is best for our pocket because, no matter what anyone says, only <u>WE</u> know what is best for us. We cannot allow outside opinions, negativity and most importantly, "the fluff"[21], alter the decision we have set in our hearts.

Bonus Feature: How to Become a Money Shark

Read "INFLUENECE: The Psychology of Persuasion." This book provides details on the psychological tactics of persuasion inside the mind. To become a shark, we

20   Blood money—referred to the act of obtaining money in a relentless manner and at a cost of suffering to others.

21   Fluff—something vacuous, such as a verbal statement, without any particular meaning or value

have to learn to put our feelings aside and focus all of our energy with the feeling of making our pockets fatter. We have to learn to become relentless with our sale tactics and learn to manipulate any person who walks past us. If we can learn to shut our heart off for this specific time, then we will be capable of earning more money than we ever imagined. Just remember, we must not *take* money, we must *earn* it.

Now, what is the best way to earn money? Simple, you earn it. We do not make money and money does not make us, so we hope. However, you need to realize that to earn money you have to be willing and determined to go through the hard times that will occur in finding our way. Those who say money is the root of all kinds of evil are usually poor, lazy, and blaming others for their unsatisfied lifestyle. In one way or another, they always seem to find an excuse for why they cannot earn a certain amount of money or do not have enough of it. If we are so unhappy with our current financial situation and want a change, then CHANGE! Why beat around the bush and sit around kicking rocks and being upset that we do not have the kind of money we want or why we only have what we have? Instead, let us change our mindset about the present and be positive. Yes, you may be unhappy, but be grateful and appreciate where it has brought you today. The money we currently have is what purchased the socks on our feet and the shirt on our back. Step back and think about the people in third world countries who do not even know what money looks like. They are sitting and picking flies off of last month's food donation and wondering when their next meal will be. Yeah, your situation looks a heck of a lot better now, right? Be happy and grateful for all the things money has done for you until now. Stop complaining because you do not have this or that, or how you wish you could have more and change your mindset for the better. Stay focused on all the positive actions money has brought your way.

> **Remember:** *You can always get rich, but finding wealth comes from within your heart and soul.*

Personal Activity #1: List three actions about money that make you aggravated. For example, your electric bill, school tuition, internet porn bills that keep reoccurring even though you cancelled (not as if I know anything about that!)

Take a look at the items that you have listed and focus all your energy on changing how you mentally feel about each one of them. Then, write down the positive factors the list has brought to you, even if it is only one thing.

> *Example: "Paying the electricity bill enables me to turn on my lights, charge my phone that I need for work, and keep the food inside my refrigerator fresh so my family and I can eat."*

_____

_____

_____

_____

Changing your mindset and feelings towards financial situations in a positive way is the hardest adjustment of all. Be that as it may, once you embrace the change, you will start to feel better and your perception of money will shed a new light. Now, you will love your money and become excited about it. So excited that you will not be able to withhold your excitement and will just want to throw it in the air, kiss it, rub it all over your genitals, and any other thing that you like to do when you are excited. Start to visualize yourself with an abundance of money, believe in it, and stay in that state of excitement. It sounds crazy, I know, but it really isn't. You need to stay in this state of excitement and positivity because as cliché as it may sound, what goes around, comes around. If you send out positive vibes and positive energy, positive energy and positive vibes will come right back to you. Eventually, you will learn that this law of attraction applies to everything in this bountiful world of ours

Tip: To better understand how the Law of Attraction works, because it is not as easy as everyone thinks it is, I recommend you watch "The Secret." This video was my stepping-stone to success.

Personal Activity #2: Write down how much you want to earn this year and be specific by narrowing it down to the tee.

Example: $179,263.00

1. _____

    By writing down this specific number, we are beginning the process of expanding our minds and opening up a completely new package of progression. This new you (the package of progression) is now confident, positive, presently visualizing a new and happy future, and letting your imagination run wild. We can now start to use our brain in a way towards money that we never thought possible; so let it happen and allow the creativity to run through your veins. Enjoy the process of visualization, capture the pictures in your mind, and remember them as vividly as the feeling.

    The next step is to choose the path in which we earn our money, but it all begins by always doing our best to stay positive, being smart, staying sharp, and enjoying the journey. When I was 17 years old, after learning I was going to repeat senior year, I changed my mindset about attending college and the school system and instead, decided to pursue a trait that would enable to me to earn money without attending school. I decided I would start cutting men's hair out of my bedroom. Of course, I had no idea how to cut hair. I had never picked up a scissor or a pair of clippers, but I was mentally set that this was the choice for me and the path I was going to take. Because I knew absolutely nothing of this field, and I mean nothing, I took the initiative to go out and ask a few people who were already successful in the hair business if they could teach me or just let me observe. After a handful of empty responses, one finally came through. This person (Manny Fernandez) showed me the ropes and six months later, I was running a full-blown barbershop in the comfort of my own bedroom and earning a weekly salary of $600 in cash. At 17, you would think that was enough, but not for me. I then decided that I would take a trip to Pennsylvania two months before July 4th, and buy a sh@t-load of fireworks to the point where the back of the borrowed pickup truck resembled a mountain. Why? Because if you took the trip early, the fireworks were RIDICULOUSLY cheap and I was going straight to the source. Example: I would purchase 12 dozen boxes of Sky Rocket Whistlers for $51.00 a box, which breaks down to a cost of $4.25 per box. Each box then contains 12-packs of Sky Rocket Whistlers, which breaks down to a cost of $0.35 per pack. I would sell each individual pack of Sky Rocket Whistlers for $2.00; $2.00 x 144 whistlers = $288.00. Basically, I quintupled my initial investment on each transaction and that was just from one dozen. Imagine all the other fireworks I had sold.

As a 17 year-old teenager with zero bills, I had found my way to earn $7,000–$8,000 in one month from the money I made selling fireworks, cutting men's hair, CD's, porn, and bootleg movies. Talk about being creative! The bigger picture here is that you have to start thinking *outside the box* and start looking at the big numbers by breaking it down from the source to see where you can make the best return on your investment. Anytime you see an item or a product, begin a habit of finding out where that person you are purchasing from got it and so on and so forth until you find the main source of productivity to expand the maximum profit for your pocket.

Remember: The best businessman is the best middleman.

Personal Activity #3 Part A: Create a list of ways you would like to earn more money, what you would like to do with the extra money, and three ways you will change your current lifestyle to achieve your desired income. But before you do that, review and analyze these two small examples:

> *Example 1: I will stop going drinking and eating at restaurants to save $525 a week until I can afford to purchase an ice cream truck so I can drive around town and sell ice cream on my days off from work.*

Do you feel like entering the ice cream business is wrong? Or a bad way to earn extra cash? Guess what? Several U.S states have deemed it illegal to carry ice cream in your back pocket and illegal to have it in your hands on a Sunday! I know, it sounds f#$%ing crazy right? Nevertheless, it is illegal in the states of Kentucky, Alabama, Oregon, and a few others to do so. Now, let us ask ourselves, is selling ice cream, the delicious and flavorful treat that everyone loves, an unethical way to earn money just because it is illegal? Most of us probably would answer, *"No, this is a perfectly good way to earn money. It's only ice cream."* Maybe it is, but compared to what?

Example 2: I will stop going out to bars and clubs so I can save $400 a week and have $1,600 at the end of the month. Now, I can purchase half a pound of marijuana and break it down into nuggets²² or one gram of marijuana, and triple my investment to earn $4,320.
Did you find this example as offensive and/or a bad way to earn money? Again, maybe it is, but to whom? As of January 2014, 21 U.S states have legalized marijuana and in 2013 over $1.43 billion worth of legal marijuana was sold between retailers, processors, and dispensaries. In the state of Colorado alone, retail owners estimated they generated over $1 million in collective sales on the FIRST day of legalization. Because of modernization, in any legalized state, we can find a dispensary on every block. So, is selling marijuana, the drug that is helping people with side effects of chemotherapy and legally generating profits for business owners, an unethical way to earn money just because it is illegal in the other half of the nation? Is this form of earning extra money, categorized as good or bad?

My point being, and hopefully you have understood the logic, money is neither good nor bad. It is just money. Moreover, because it is just money, we also cannot become its hostage and let it act as a puppet master. When money controls the actions or reactions that take place in our lives, then money is in control. If money purchases items that are poisonous to our bodies, then money is in control. When money causes us to degrade ourselves as human beings and negatively change our mindset where we disable ourselves to grow, then money is in control. These are the *real evils* of money. Not the money itself, but what we do with it. Once money is in our hands, we should not use it to create a harmful lifestyle to ourselves or others. Only through our minds, hearts, and positive

22   Nuggets—something small but valuable

spirits are we aware of the best ways to use our money because as long as we are honest with ourselves and use it for the greater good, will we know how to create the lifestyle we wish to achieve. If money enhances our positive lifestyle, then we control money. If we choose to donate our money to the sick and needy, then we control our money. If it is used to uplift ourselves spiritually as human beings, then we control our money. When it is spent to help us become that much closer to our goals, then we control our money.

So, how are you going to earn your money, what are you going to do with it, and how will you change your current lifestyle to achieve your desired income?

_____

_____

_____

_____

_____

_____

Personal Activity #3 Part B: Now that you know what money will do for you, list the ways you will change your inner-self to be in control of money.

Examples:

- I will change my perception of money and will not judge how it is earned.

- I will now respect money for its power to enhance who I am in a positive way.

- I will now have a positive emotional attachment to money.

_____

_____

_____

_____

_____

In conclusion, money is just money and it will only become evil based upon the manner in which it is controlled. If it controls us, then we are the ones who are evil. If we control it, then we have won the first battle in bettering our lifestyle and becoming a better us.

STACK 8

CREATIVITY

"Creativity is intelligence having fun."
– Albert Einstein

Have you ever found yourself in a moment where you admired somebody for his or her creativity and said, "Wow, I wish I could be like that" or felt inferior because you do not think you have the potential to be "as creative" as he or she is. Well, shame on you for not believing in yourself! Inside all of us, there lies an untapped world of creativity just waiting to be unleashed with ideas ready to come to life. Many of us do not realize that we all have a special connection inside our minds that can produce creativity. Some know how to tap into this special talent and know how and when to apply it, while others have no idea or even believe they are creative at all because as soon as they hear the word "creative", they automatically think about art, graphic design, music, etc. We all perceive creativity to be a physical act that can only be made with the use of tools in an "artistic manner." Wrong. This example is only *one* of the *many* forms creativity truly is. Being creative is about expressing your inner thoughts and bringing those thoughts into reality. Being creative is about using knowledge, imagination, and inner power to create something new and valuable to the world. Creativity is limitless and there is no right or wrong way to express it. We are our own leaders of creativity. And only we know the best ways to get the most out of it.

Being creative is not a trait that only a few carry. It is a special power that we all possess because it is a way of thinking, a way of acting, and a way of living. Every one of us was brought into this world to create. The difference is that we are not all born with the same type of creativity. Deep inside, everybody has their own way of being creative and using it in different degrees, different angles, different levels, different aspects, different procedures, and just plain . . . different. Every creative mind is different in style and objective. Therefore there really is no true label as to what creativity is simply because the approach is limitless.

What kind of creative power do you possess? Through what "creative eye" do you express yourself? Is it through:

o *Improvisation*—The creative process where words are delivered in a verbal, composed, or written manner. These are ideas expressed without preparation, developed at the person's own creative free will, and generate new ways to act and think on the spot. It helps to enhance our instinctive reactions when asked certain questions, helps during live performances, and helps our intuition quicken to pull the trigger on making decisions at any given moment. This creative aspect enables our minds to let loose, run wild, be free with our thoughts, and put all of our ideas into action. Improvisation withholds the key to the adventure of stepping into the unknown. Musicians, athletes, painters/artists, writers, actors, etc. usually display this type of creativity.

Example: Eminem is great at improvisation because he can rap at any given moment and make sense of his words, make them rhyme, and provide great delivery (100% my opinion).

o   **Innovative and Adaptive**—When we enter the adaptive creative mindset, it usually takes place during a present scenario that needs to be resolved immediately. During this creative mindset, we must learn to embrace our current situation and adjust to create a better future within the respective field to produce the desired outcome. This creative action helps the mind be innovative and add bright new ideas to thoughts that already existed. This skill is normally seen in product inventors, office managers, or people in a structured environment where discipline, systematic procedures, structure, and formatted applications are the methods of creative approach.

Example: This weed is too plain and not selling. I will sprinkle a little crack inside the product and name it "The Wu Banger" to create something different and generate more sales.

Those are only a couple of examples on how to approach creativity. So, which creative approach do you currently use or wish to use? It doesn't matter which one it is, the objective is to find a way to let the creative juices flow. Every position in life is a new opportunity to be creative, to start thinking of new ways to do things, letting our minds open up to new visualizations and allowing ourselves to take any idea, wild or not, into physical form. If we are the manager of a restaurant and no one is coming to the bar on Friday nights, we must find creative ways to attract customers. If we are on a public toilet and run out of toilet paper, we must get creative to clean our butts. If we are a painter and run out of red acrylic paint with no money to buy more, we must get creative to make a similar color or choose a different theme. No matter the scenario, we must open our minds to new ideas and allow those creative thoughts to come to life. So, how creative are you?

How to Activate or Enhance Our Creative Minds

How we activate and enhance our creative minds is the biggest question. For starters, just *thinking* how to become more creative is a great first step to begin activating creative brainwaves to begin flowing into action. Writing, cooking, exercising, rapping in front of a mirror to your favorite Wu-Tang Clan song, singing and zoning out to your favorite song in the car, or masturbating are some of the many different ways that one can express their creative thoughts. Perform any activity that will put the mind at ease and enables you to think clearly, or, as Chubbs in Happy Gilmore would say, "Go to your happy place." Everybody has a happy place where they can mentally go to be completely relaxed, put a smile on their face, and doesn't force any thoughts. Forcing thoughts will only lead us into creative destruction because it is not our true thought; it was influenced by the force of thinking rather than the flow of thinking. When we achieve going to our happy place, our minds are able to open up and allow creative thoughts to process without interruption.

Likewise, we must also physically put ourselves in a comfortable atmosphere where we may be alone with our thoughts. The less distracted we are, the easier it will be to get into a certain flow. We must place ourselves in quiet and peaceful settings such as parks, beaches, bedrooms, going for walks, sitting in our cars, or any places of preference where there will be no outside interference. Once our mind and body are at ease, the creative brainwaves will start to activate because it will only be our thoughts and us.

Here are three mental exercises to perform that will help bring awareness to our creativity:

1. Get Crazy

In case you have not paid attention to your inner self, *we are our own worst enemy.* There are outside distractions such as opinions, people, media, etc., but the main distraction, the king of kings, is our own "voice of reason." Anytime we think of a great idea and the success it may bring, that little voice of reason automatically jumps in and pummels the idea with a zillion excuses of why it would never work: "What kind of a stupid idea is that?!", "Are you out of your mind?! You have no time for that!", "That idea is terrible, what are you thinking!", "How does that even make sense?!", "Everyone will think you are crazy!", "Just quit now!" Put a muzzle on that voice of reason and allow yourself to step into the unknown. Take a ride on the wild side! Yes, breaking what is considered "normal" makes us crazy, but that is exactly what we need to become creative. We must step out of the norm! Yes, the thoughts may sound crazy, but that is what creative people operate! The thoughts only seem crazy because they are different from everyone else's and different from what we normally think.

These are a few examples of some "crazy" people who changed our world:

o   In the 1800's John and Will Kellogg "paved the way for a whole new era in the land of breakfast" with their creation of Corn Flakes, beginning the brand that maintains its dedication to quality still today. Dr. John Kellogg believed Corn Flakes, the cheap and somewhat bland but tasty cereal, would be the solution to "what was eating away at society and destroying all that was good in the world." "He believed a simple diet low in sugar would be paramount in preventing little children from masturbating." (Pause for laughter) However, his brother, Will Kellogg, was crazy enough to believe otherwise and created Frosted Flakes.[23]

o   Yoshiro Nakamatsu is a Japanese inventor who currently holds the most patents in history with a total exceeding 4,000 and is best known for inventing the CD, DVD, taxicab meter, and digital watch. These, among his other inventions, result from his belief that his creativity process works at its best when there is a lack of oxygen to the brain. He often holds his breath underwater until 0.5 seconds before potential death using a "special waterproof Plexiglas writing pad [he] invented."[24]

o   In 1903, inventors and aviators worldwide believed the Wright Brothers were crazy when

23,24   "The Top 10 Crazy Bastards Who Actually Changed The World (For The Better)" <www.spike.com>

their aeronautical work to solve the then-present flying problem was centered on developing an accurate pilot control system instead of building the "ultimate engine" like everyone else was. A few years later, the Wright Brothers successfully developed the first aircraft control that enabled pilots to steer and maintain balance. This remains the standard for all fixed-winged aircrafts today.[25]

o It took Entertainment Company Rovio Entertainment Ltd 51 games before launching their global slingshot-puzzle game, number-one-hit-sensation Angry Birds, achieving over two billion global downloads and over 200 million active users every month. Initially, Chief Marketing Officer Peter Vesterbacka believed he was "super ambitious in 2010 [one year after the official Angry Bird launch] when [he] said [to the company they would] make $100 million and everyone thought [he] was crazy, but [felt it was] very important people thought [he] was insane for saying $100 million back then."—Rovio's revenue in 2013 totaled €156 million[26] or roughly USD$200 million.

You see, creative people often have more bad ideas than good ones. The difference is that creative people step

---

25   "Angry Birds: PG Connects: Rovio's Vesterbacka: They called me crazy–now Angry Birds rivals Coke" <www.mobile-ent.biz>

26   Rovio Entertainment Reports 2013 Financial Results <www.rovio.com>

into the crazy and take action on each idea. Therefore, the answer to that ever-pressing question that runs around in our minds is "No, we are not crazy. We are being creative." We must act on those irregular thoughts that run through our heads and do things the average human being would not do. We must become so crazy to believe we can actually accomplish what we dream of from the start. We cannot let the little voices in our heads slow us down from creating what we wish to have, because feeling out of place is what happens during a new creation. Feeling out of place is scary. However, once people start thinking you are crazy for your actions, that is when you know you are going in the right direction.

2. Attack at Will

Ready, Aim, Fire! Always move forward when you are ready to move forward. While it feels good to have the reassurance, consent, opinions, and the outside perspectives of others, it yields no results for us or our creative tactics. Listening to what others think about our creative process will only slow down progression. We need to learn to take outside opinions with as small a grain of salt as possible because a majority of the time, the outside opinion is geared towards their own personal preference. The outside opinion is not part of our original creative process, hence why it is called an outside opinion. If we let others influence our original thoughts, we are allowing them to steer us towards an unwanted path. Like my childhood friend Brian Davis says, "Sometimes in our path, there are forks in the road. Either you must choose to go right or left, but no matter which direction we choose to go, it was our original thought and not someone else's. By listening to an outside opinion meant we chose the path of destruction by heading straight towards the fork and smashing into the divider." So, let us always remind ourselves that we must move forward at our own will and no one else's. Never wait for reassurance that "you are doing the right thing" because it will only halt your creative process. Should you encounter someone who wants to interrupt the free-flowing, productive, and creative path you have chosen, tell him or her to f@#k off. Who are they to interfere with your creativity?

Remember: *Always remind yourself "This is the creative path that I have chosen and anyone who dares to get in the way of my process will get shoved, smashed, and burned on the shoulder on my creative road."*

3. Let's Be Honest

The freedom of a creative mindset delivers an extremely meaningful process and a very valuable voyage in our lives. As such, we must approach the creative process with a certain sense of care, awareness, and logic. Logic brings the most important and grandest tool we will ever learn in life: Honesty. During the creative process, we must consider the action we are willing to take and honestly ask ourselves if they are the correct moves that will enhance our lifestyle. For example, if you are the general manager of the New York Knicks your job is to put together a great team, coaching staff, and assign the appropriate job positions within the company. The coaching staff will create the plays for execution in the game, the players will execute the created plays for the game with their own style, and each staff member will organize and create a comfortable, stable atmosphere for the players and the coaches so they can win games. As you can see, in each position there is a certain responsibility as well as level of creativity that must be upheld. As the general manager, you hold an even greater responsibility since you are in charge of facilitating an atmosphere that enables others to be creative. Have you hired the correct coaches? Have you drafted the correct teammates to flow with the atmosphere of the franchise? Have you assigned the correct responsibilities to the designated people? For the general manager, these are questions that must be answered with true honesty, and if you are honest, your creation will show both on the court and the scoreboard.

To be effective with the creation we have put together we must be accurate with our decisions, and that accuracy comes from honesty. As long as you honestly believe in the creative process, then there is no reason why you should second-guess your actions. To succeed with creativity, we must be honest with where we stand in relation to our goals. For example, if you are a 4-foot Asian with a vertical leap of 3 inches, it would be honest to say that you should not set your creative goals towards playing for the New York Knicks (but then again there was Jeremy Lin . . . see do not let outside opinions interfere if you believe you can make it). We must ask ourselves and respond truthfully, "Have I taken enough time to acquire the required skills?", "Are the goals I have set truly what I want in life?", "Do I have what it takes to become legendary?", and "Am I willing to become crazy enough to be successful in this aspect of life?" Be humble with your creative actions and always be aware that every time a task or goal is accomplished, there is always room for growth. Just because you have no idea about the subject, it does not mean it is unattainable. Just start where you are now and watch yourself grow into a creation your mind and body never knew existed.

Personal Activity #1:

1. Choose one thing you do every day that you will eliminate from your life in order to make time to visit "your happy place."

_____

_____

_____

2. Write down a time and place where you can be alone and comfortable.

_____

_____

_____

3. Choose a task to start exercising your creative mind set.

_____

_____

_____

Observe the tactic you have chosen, this is the approach that you believe will be the best method to enhance your creative mindset. Be sure to perform this exercise every day until it becomes a habit and eventually, an instinct. Only by clearing the mind and allowing the natural flow of thoughts will we be able to activate the creative world lying inside.

Personal Activity #2: Be creative and draw/scribble a picture of where you would like to see yourself one year from now. Be honest and keep this picture as a reminder of what you are striving for. Remember, this is your own personal mental picture so it does not matter what it looks like, just go with the flow.

Why Be Creative

The voyage the creative process brings is one we should all experience with nothing but excitement. Stepping out of the everyday life in order to create something new and innovative to change the world is the utmost personal experience we should all consider having in order to succeed. I am not telling you to go out and find the cure for cancer (unless that is your goal), but do something out of the ordinary. Expand your thoughts through the exercise of creation and allow yourself to travel into another mindset you never believed you could achieve. Be crazy enough to perform at levels the average world has never seen. Take honest risks in life to enhance the mind, body, and soul and always try something new with your thoughts to put together a different picture in your mind. We must strike at our own will with no second-guessing our actions. We must live and think freely, but act with care. We must act instinctively, but with honesty. We must change the world inside and around us with one creative thought at a time. That is creativity.

Lights; Camera; Action!

If we see the brighter light within ourselves and this visualization and creativity are what have the cameras rolling, then what are we waiting for? Are we waiting for an open invitation? No! It is time for us to take some M@#$3R-FU%$!NG ACTION!

Let us start playing the lead role in our own movie. It is time for us to shine the spotlight on ourselves because we have now chosen to become bigger, better, and stronger than our old selves beginning a new journey. All of our knowledge is stocked, locked, and loaded inside our minds and prepared to blast off like a 14-year-old kid getting dry humped for hours at the school dance during a reggae song. We are all aware of what procedures will get us closer to our dreams. We have everything written down, each task is mentally pictured, and the scenarios are visualized; all that is left is to pull the trigger and blast off! It is time of us to take those thoughts and put them into action so that we can create the physical life we wish to achieve. Without action, our thoughts will simply stay as thoughts, collect dust, and never enter the physical world. By taking action on our thoughts, we begin to realize what *will* and *will not* work towards the goals we have set. Action will help us build a strong filtration system inside ourselves to recognize and eliminate the negative actions and proceed only with the positive actions. As so, every action we take must be an action we wholeheartedly believe in and is an action that will only create what we are striving for in life.

How many times have we said to ourselves or heard someone else say, "That was my idea!" or "I thought about that before!" Well, what are words going to do for us? It is time to put those words to rest and take action so we do not become a member of that infamous group of people who always have a great idea but never go through with it. We do not want to be *"that guy."* Creating an idea is the easy part, 99.99% of people have developed a great idea, but have never put the idea into action because it is too hard. They do not want to go through the hard work nor have the dedication, the willingness to sacrifice, or the balls to take action and bring the idea to fruition. They are scared of not knowing the outcome, so when they finally find a small amount of courage to move forward with their idea, they quit halfway because it became too hard and/or too confusing. Plain and simple: They just do not want to get off their f#$%ing asses and do what it takes to taste success. They just want to say they had an idea, talk about it with others, and dwell on and on about the idea never being able to become a reality. Not us, pal! We are not part of that 99.99% who give up and/or become lazy. We are not a punk ass mofo. We are part of the elite 0.01% that actually wants success. Yes, I am sure we might have all been in that place at one point or another or maybe are living in this way of life now. So no, I am not trying to knock us down because I am sure everyone is trying their best to the extent of their own awareness. But we are better than that. Let others be themselves and let us stay focused on our own personal and positive actions and not let other people's actions and negativity interfere or affect our own. Just do you, kid!

Action and Reaction

"For every action, there is an equal and opposite reaction"—Issac Newton

The above quote refers to Issac Newton's Third Law of Motion. Now, as stated before, I am not here to give a science lesson, but we do need to become aware of how relevant this law is in relationship to the actions we take in life. Let us break down the law a little: For every action we take, we are reinforcing a specific reaction. The type of reaction received, whether positive or negative, will be dependent on the type of action we take. Any interference will cause the reaction to be "pulled" in two different directions and will only go in the desired direction if a greater momentum is created. What does this all mean? There is cause and effect for all of our actions. Our actions may not go as smoothly as we planned or intended, but it is up to us to change them and keep moving towards the direction we choose.

In order to get down to business, we have to start using the "ACT AS IF" method. We must "fake it until we make it" because it is a great way to force our actions to be more optimistic and begin altering our minds so that we slowly build our confidence and genuineness. The more we "ACT AS IF" with our actions, the sooner it will become habitual and will eventually be who we really are. Of course, our actions will feel fugazi at first, but if we stay consistent with this method, we will begin to notice that the reactions received have changed into positive feedback towards achieving our goals. As Jim Young in Boiler Room (2000) said, "Act as if. You understand what that means? Act as if you are the fucking President of this firm. Act as if you got a 9" cock. Okay? Act as if." This method is very powerful and life changing for us all. If we understand the logic of action and reaction, what do you think will happen if we approach each action with the intent of positivity? Correct, positive actions will create positive reactions. With positive action and positive reactions, we will build an additional momentum of positive attraction towards our goals. It is easy to create positive thoughts, especially the kind filled with sunshine and rainbows, but how can we convert those positive thoughts into actions and how can we apply that positivity towards everyday life? Have you ever heard that saying, "Actions speak louder than words?" Well, if we are looking for a positive change in our lives, we must deeply consider that saying.

Here are some simple tactics that will help our actions build momentum in the right direction by receiving the correct reaction and allow us to take another step closer to our goals.

> o **Smile**—For crying aloud, SMILE! Whether you have real teeth, fake teeth, gold teeth, rotten teeth, or no teeth, just smile! It doesn't even matter if you are upset about something, just put a smile on your face and refuse to show the world that you are unhappy. This small action will more than likely attract the reaction you are looking for. If you approach a stranger and you're ice grillin'[27] them as if you were a Blood walking into Crypt territory, then it is pretty obvious you will not be welcomed with open arms and receive the reaction you were looking for. (For the record, I do not suggest anyone to walk through Blood or Crypt territory.

27   Ice grillin'—a slang term to define giving an individual a mean and cold facial expression.

The only reaction you will get is being shot in the forehead.) Now, if you approach a stranger with a nice and genuine smile, it is highly likely that you will be receiving a smile back. This reciprocated smile just opened up the door for the reaction we are seeking because that person now feels comfortable and open to communication. You never know, you could have just brightened their day with your smile.

o **Strut**—Walk around like your sh!t don't stink! I am not saying to get cocky or think you are the best person to walk the face of the Earth, but begin to develop some confidence in the way you present yourself. Match that Colgate smile of yours by walking the streets with your back straight, chest puffed out a little, head forward, and your chin slightly tilted up. These small changes will boost your confidence and create a much more approachable look to those around you. We cannot walk around like the Hunchback of Notre Dame and expect to receive the reactions we want. Additionally, as cliché as it may sound, we also need to clean up and take care of ourselves as well. We need to put on nice clothes, get good haircuts, brush our teeth, get in good shape, or simply just take a shower! We have to be presentable and look and feel good about ourselves to have that extra boost to receive the reactions we seek. Now, let us be honest with ourselves, would you approach yourself? If the answer is no, then what can you change about yourself to appear more presentable and approachable?

Take action and make those changes. If you answered yes, then you are just a cocky bastard because there is always something we can change about ourselves. If you still think otherwise and believe there is nothing to change about your current presentation, then close this book up and wipe you're a$$ with it because you are obviously too good for this crap!

o   *Gestures*—Begin to start acting upon small gestures to help others. Saying thank you, complimenting someone on their outfit, telling people to have a great day, making jokes and laughing with complete strangers, donating money to the right people or foundations, or simply placing the shopping cart back where it belongs are some of the many actions that can make a difference. However, you must be genuine and sincere. Do not fluff a person's feathers with positive words and/or actions if you do not sincerely mean it and are doing it just to make yourself feel better. **We must first be able to look in the mirror with confidence, stare through our eyes with inspiration, and speak our words with honesty. In doing so, we will be able to spread the true characteristics we have acquired with positive actions and receive positive reactions. Also, be aware that some people may not react the way you expect them too. Some may brush you off or think you are crazy. More than likely, this will be the case but do not be quick to slam down your gavel and be quick to judge them. Everyone has a different**

mindset and everyone has a different level of awareness.

"SAY CHEESE!"

Keep in mind that trying to change someone else's way of life will only inflict more stress on us. Therefore, it is best to move forward, continue with our positive actions and gestures, and strut on with our sparkling smile.

These are only some small suggestions and actions for, what I believe are very beneficial ways, to generate positive reactions. Everyone is different and may have different methods on how to inspire joys within themselves, and that is okay.

In essence, we need to start putting our thoughts into actions. We need to truly believe in them so we can start receiving the reactions we truly seek. If you're still unsure of how to begin, start with a smile. Surely a smile never hurt anyone.

Remember: *Expect Less and Achieve More.*

Personal Activity #1: List down the thoughts we are going to start putting action towards.

Examples:

- I am going to smile at the girl I always see on the train, and approach her if she smiles back.

- I am going to pound my chest like a gorilla and scream at the top of my lungs every morning to start my day with confidence and release any stress I may have.

_____

_____

_____

_____

_____

_____

_____

_____

_____

_____

_____

_____

Effective Actions

Going that extra mile with our actions will allow us to explore different opportunities. Whether it is at work, the practice room, the gym, or even your own business, start pushing yourself to do a little more than usual. By doing more than usual, we will see an affect on our actions and begin to notice a difference inside of us and our surroundings. Our effective actions will make us feel much more accomplished than normal and will allow us to separate ourselves from the pack because others will take notice of the extra work being done. It will also show that we take our field seriously and are willing to go that extra mile to get the job done correctly and/or better than usual. When others recognize the effects of our actions, it actually means we are leaving a mark in their memory. When a moment presents itself and they need something done in the specific field we previously acted on, our actions will be the first thing that pops into their mind. When the respect for our quality and quantity of our actions is given, we will begin to advance in our field and fly past those who are sitting down and scratching their asses. On the contrary, if the actions of our hard work are not acknowledged or met with respect, it is unfortunate to say, but you are in the wrong environment. When you truly believe the actions you are producing are extremely effective, and nothing has changed after being patient, then this is a sign that it is time to change your environment. If you truly believe in your craft and the effectiveness of your craft and actions, then stick with what you know and believe in, and continue going that extra mile instead of following the crowd. By going that extra mile, we are proving to ourselves that we have the determination and focus inside of us to do what it takes to achieve the reactions we deserve.

"Don't wait to strike till the iron is hot, but make the iron hot by striking . . ."—William B. Sprague

Qualities Needed to Develop Personal Power

Making our thoughts come to action and making our actions be effective is no walk in the park. It takes a certain type of mentality, personality, tenacity, and physical being in order to have our actions come to reality. In other words, it takes personal power. Personal power is not about how much weight we can bench press or how many squats we can do. As Kenny Powers said, "I ain't trying to be the best in exercising!" Personal power is about how we use our knowledge, how we use our thoughts, how we use our feelings, and how we encourage all of these emotions to meet or respond in a positive fashion. Personal power is a trait we can all develop as long as we are willing to meet its demand of determination, will, integrity, courage, discipline, and most importantly, action.

o   *Self-determination: Making a decision*—This is a self-motivational action that requires one to come to a conclusive decision and stick with it. The quality of our determination will be based on how strong we can make our mind be to enable us to move forward without any past concerns or doubts about the outcome. With self-determination, we can develop the inner strength to "put our foot down" and proceed without caution. If we are determined, then we will never give up. Determination will help us remind ourselves what our goal is, why we are doing such tasks, and help us push past our expectations.

   Example: I will not stop trying to throw punches at my opponent until the fight is over so I can better my chance of winning.

o   *Willpower: Self-discipline*—This is a great avenue for self-improvement because it will help us break old habits and not create new ones. Willpower is the mental adjustment to hold back on our natural instincts that will lead us to fall into any temptations that stop our progress. By developing strong willpower, we are developing the power to control and block our thoughts and emotions from receiving influences by outside forces and causing us discomfort. This power is not an action of strength or weakness, yet it is a power of self-consciousness where one is able to stay relaxed and calm in a natural mind state during rough times.

Example: Ms. Parker from next-door keeps watering her plants while wearing a see-through shirt on and I know she is doing it on purpose. I will contain myself from engaging with her because I am married.

o **Courage: Time to strike**—You need to have balls/guts for this one because this is not for the weak and requires heart, determination, and willpower to move forward. Courage is the ability to step into our "danger zone" and walk through scenarios that frighten us. With this action, we have to mentally dig deep and find a new inner strength that our bodies and mind have never encountered. By continually putting ourselves into uncharted waters and those moments that often cause us discomfort will build our mental endurance. We must embrace those experiences that frighten us in order to learn, progress, and become stronger to face bigger tasks. If you face your fears with enough courage, your fears will become a joke in no time.

Example: I will ride every roller coaster at Six Flags to get over my fear of death from amusement park rides.

o ***Integrity: Loyalty to our values***—This action
is the self-power of being able to stay consistent throughout the progress until we reach
a certain level of success. Committing to our
methods of actions will enable us to receive
the proper outcome of the goals we have set
for ourselves. This is an ethical procedure that
requires staying honest to ourselves and the
world and building the truthfulness that will
measure the accuracy of our growing character. It means being internally consistent to
our principles on the actions we have set for
ourselves, believing in our thoughts, standing firm behind our actions, and allowing the
truth of our goals to unravel. Outside opinions
and past outcomes cannot interfere with any
of our positive beliefs and values we strongly
feel about or love.

*Example: Many people tell me that I am too old
to fight and my record sucks. Despite all the distractions, I will keep fighting because I love the
sport and it makes me a stronger person mentally and physically.*

o ***Discipline: Code of conduct***—This is the ability to give ourselves an order and go through the
process until the desired outcome is achieved.
A disciplined person is someone who is determined to accomplish a goal and has the willpower to achieve it by moving forward with
courage at any expense of his/her own integrity. To achieve self-discipline, we must develop
the ability to control any negative or doubtful

feelings to overcome/strengthen any weakness we may feel. This action is the ability to pursue what we believe in and reject any temptations that could persuade us to abandon our goals. True discipline will give us the self-power over our own lives.

Example: I will stop drinking, smoking weed and cigarettes, and having sex with useless women to keep my mind sharp and intact with my goals. I will give up all distractions, certain friends, parties, events, and anything that will alter my thoughts or slow down my process until I am a multi-millionaire.

So what have we learned? For every action we take, there will be a reciprocating reaction. For every reaction, there will be a cause. For every cause, there will be an effect. For every effect, there will be a response. For every response, there will be an outcome. For every outcome, there will be an adjustment. For every adjustment, there will be a new action. Rinse, wash, and repeat until we are successful, because success is not for lightweights. Achieving our personal success is not an easy fight to train for because it will not fall from the sky and into our lap. We have to prepare properly and train our mind and body for the hard times to be able to push through them when things get rough. We can achieve this mental and physical toughness through one procedure at a time; and that procedure is called ACTION. Everyone has a "million dollar idea" but no one wants to take the million steps it takes to get there. So let us ask ourselves: Do we really want success? Do we have what it takes? Do we want to live an extraordinary life? Then it is time to get off our lazy asses, start playing the lead role in our own movie, and become the action hero that we are!

> **Remember:** *Easier said than done, but once it is done, it is that much easier.*

EXPERIENCE

We Gain Knowledge About Ourselves Through Experience

"I don't believe people are looking for the meaning of life as much as they are looking for the experience of being alive." —Joseph Campbell

We have not witnessed diddlysquat[28] until we experience the situation ourselves. We learn the most through experience. The more we experience, the more we will understand our meaning and purpose in life. We can read all the books in the world, gather up all the information we know and have learned, watch countless movies and documentaries, but what good will any of that do if we fail to use it? What good will any of it do if we have yet to step into the world we perceive and never achieve the world we believe? The real knowledge, wisdom, and success is learned when we undergo specific experiences by putting our best foot forward when walking through the fire. Yes, we will lose, we will fail, things will go wrong, we will f#@k up, we will get hurt, and we will be burned during our fight to reach higher limits. But that is the risk we have to be willing to take in order to achieve success! This is all part

---

28   Diddlysquat—not in the least bit

of the journey in entering a higher level of consciousness. We must be determined to face the bad experiences in order to fulfill the good ones because if we are able to withstand the rough times, we will be rewarded at the end of the journey. Remember that there is no reward without risk. We must stick to our goals and never walk away with excuses. Quit being timid, fragile and scared inside and live each and every experience. It is these experiences where we will develop a stronger foundation within us to help us reach the goals we wish to achieve, understand the fact and flaws of life, and learn how to adjust and adapt for better or worse. With every experience, we can gain confidence to move forward to the next experience and increase the confidence we already have about our goals. That being said, what is to stop us? What can stop us if we stick to our goals, accept each experience for what they are, understand what the new knowledge gained, and never ever f#$king give up? Nothing. For we have entered the limitless world of success. Once we are able to understand that true success does not have an ending and is only part of the many journeys we are to experience in life, will we realize that success isn't merely just a goal, it is also a *lifestyle*.

Until Death Do You Part

"It's better to die standing on my feet, than to live a lifetime on my knees"—Emilio Zapata

Have you ever caught yourself asking the world, "Is there anything in this life that is guaranteed?" Maybe your job wasn't guaranteed because you just got fired. Your relationship wasn't guaranteed, you found that out when it ended. Those new $800 tires you just put on your car weren't guaranteed like the salesman said, you have two flats in the front. So what is?! Well, here is the one guarantee we all share: We will all die. Nothing else in our lives is guaranteed besides the fact that the Grim Reaper (death) will eventually come knocking on our doorsteps. Death is the one and only guarantee we have in life because everything else is based off beliefs, values, trust, systems, and faith. Like Apollo Creed said, "THERE IS NO TOMORROW!" Our physical forms are not immortal. We will never know when, how, or why our death will happen, it *just does*. It just happens and there is nothing me, you, or anybody else can do about it.

Personal Activity #1: If you knew death was coming to our door in three days, what would you do? Who would you approach and why? Where would go to live your last days? With this in mind, list the three things you would do if you only had 72 hours to live. Make sure they are positivity-enhancing experiences and not situations that will diminish your value in life.

1. _____
   _____
   _____

2. _____
   _____
   _____

3. _____
   _____
   _____

Ok, did you really sit down, take your time and think about those three things? Are these the things you would like to experience before your time is up in this world? If so, then why are you not doing them now? What is stopping you from doing the things you have listed? I know right now you are coming up with a handful of reasons as to why you can't but *would* do them if you only had a few days to left to live. Let us call a spade a spade and call bulls@#t, you and I both know that those are all *excuses*. All those thoughts that ran through your head were nothing but thoughts of fear. Fear is for the weak, excuses are for those who are scared of confrontation, and we do not want any of that as part of our life experience. The truth behind the kind of experience you *truly* seek lies in that list you just made. So now here is some food for thought: Why is it that we cannot experience the life that we want if we know we are going to die eventually? Many of us fear death because we know it is for sure and do not know what happens after. Yes, there are many faith and trust-related theories and assumptions, but in reality, we really don't know what occurs because we have not experienced death itself. Therefore, it is through my perspective that we all do not really fear death, we fear stepping into the unknown. Stepping into the unknown has the same mental impact on all of us as the thought of dying does. We fear the experience of entering another dimension we are unfamiliar with and leaving behind the world we felt comfortable in living. How do we face this fear? We must die and kill our old selves so that we may come back to life and start a new journey with a fresh approach. Now, I am not saying to try to kill yourself and have an out of body experience to see if you go to heaven and come back, but understand that we must reinvent ourselves. We must face death each time and enter, as the Ultimate Warrior would say, "Parts Unknown", to grow as spiritual human beings and experience as much as life has to offer us. It is time to step out of monotony and live life as we wish to. It is time for us to live beyond our beliefs and expectations so we may all witness the ultimate experience of life. So, the next time someone asks what you might do with only 72 hours to live, you can confidently answer, "I would do exactly what I already have planned for the next 72-hours." Our job in life is not to settle for the same-old but instead to be our own witness to the experiences we dreamt of. Why not? We are all going to die anyway, right?

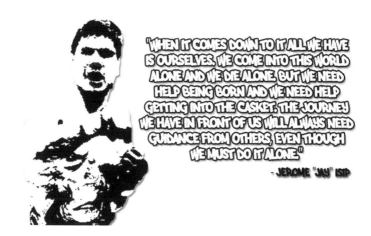

"WHEN IT COMES DOWN TO IT ALL WE HAVE IS OURSELVES. WE COME INTO THIS WORLD ALONE AND WE DIE ALONE. BUT WE NEED HELP BEING BORN AND WE NEED HELP GETTING INTO THE CASKET. THE JOURNEY WE HAVE IN FRONT OF US WILL ALWAYS NEED GUIDANCE FROM OTHERS, EVEN THOUGH WE MUST DO IT ALONE."

- JEROME "JAY" ISIP

"Rhythm is gonna get you"—Gloria Estefan

The rhythm of life is something that is tough to grasp. We all want to walk to the beat of our drum, but how do we develop it? During our life experiences, we have to develop awareness of the law of rhythm, which is what goes up must come down, and what goes down must come up. This particular concept requires a mountain of patience because in order to understand the rhythm of life, we need to be patient with the highs and the lows, the great times and the bad, and the losses and gains life will bring our way. When the rhythm of life is as its peak, we must ride that wave as long as possible, simply enjoy the experience, and not worry or wonder when it is going to end. Now, when the wave is down in rhythm, we must be patient and adjust to the best of our ability but still enjoy the experience for the knowledge it brings us. By understanding the idea that when life is down and must, in time, come back up, we can develop a sense of calmness within until things are better. Likewise, when life is up we must develop the patience to mentally prepare ourselves for when things are going to be on the down side. This is not a science lesson on the law of gravity, but a concept we must be aware of in life so we can be consciously ready for the waves that come our way. My friend Timmy Hands once told me, "Think about it this way, the rhythm of life is comparable to the actions of a surfer. A surfer paddles his way into the water and waits for a nice wave to ride. They ride the first wave, don't wipe out, and return back to paddling for the next wave. The next one unfortunately wipes him out, but what does he do? He gets back on the board and paddles into the water for the next wave." The rhythm of life is exactly like a surfer and the waters of Earth. There is always going to be a low tide and there is always going to be a high tide, but only surfers know which waves they will want to ride and which waves they should stay away from. Even when they may wipe out, they still get back on their surfboard with the intent of riding the next wave and enjoy the experience, regardless of the outcome. In other words, everything in life has a rhythm. We must know when to hit the gas, when to hit the brakes, and even when to leave it in neutral. But never ever put it in reverse because we don't want to burn ourselves out or not do enough. Just dance with the flow.

*"The world ain't all sunshine and rainbows. It's a
very mean and nasty place, and I don't care how
tough you are, it will beat you to your knees and
keep your there permanently if you let it. You, me,
or nobody is gonna hit as hard as life. But it ain't
about how hard you hit, it's about how hard you
can get hit and keep moving forward; how much
you can take and keep moving forward. That's how
winning is done! Now, if you know what you're
worth, then go out and get what you're worth.
But you gotta be willing to take the hits, and not
pointing fingers saying you ain't where you wanna
be because of him, or her, or anybody. Cowards do
that and that ain't you! You're better than that!"*
– Rocky Balboa (2006)

The Four Aces of Life

Every experience in life can be broken down into four separate segments that we all go through. We must become aware of these four aspects in life so that we can properly deal with these experiences to the best of our ability, making the process of exploring our paths much easier.

1. Appreciation—I am not trying to sound redundant here, but we must appreciate *all* of the experiences we have faced. The truth is, whether the experience was positive or negative, it will never come our way again. So, appreciate each experience for all the new knowledge, new strength, and new wisdom we gained from them, for it has made us into the person we are today.

2. Acceptance—The power of acceptance is a strong attribute for our present mind state. By accepting the facts and flaws of who we are today, we will enable ourselves to not hold grudges on our past experiences. Accepting who and what we are in life today will only open the new doors for tomorrow. Accept and understand that we must not expect anything from anyone any situation, but rather just accept life for what it is. The only expectation we can have in life, is life itself. We have heard this saying many times, but the meaning is true, everything that happens in our lives, happens for a reason. Every experience in our lives serves a purpose and all that we can do is accept life for what it is, and what our life is not. Accept the present and only expect life to come in its own fashion.

3. Adjustment—Simple changes in our present lives will adjust the future. After accepting the present, we must make adjustments in our lives to enter the new doors we have just opened. In order to move forward with our actions, we must mentally adjust and prepare ourselves to erase our fears and step into the unknown. During this transitional stage of adjustment, our minds and bodies will fight each other and attempt to hold us back from proceeding. Each time we feel the struggle of doubt and fear, we have to continuously adjust our mindsets and remain focused on the bigger picture. As said before, whether a positive or negative experience, we must mentally adjust all of our thoughts into positive ones so we can enter our new journey smoother.

4. Adaptation—We have appreciated the past, accepted the present, and made adjustments to enter the future, so now it is time to adapt to the new journey we have chosen. We have to adapt to the new experiences we will face and mold ourselves into the new environment we have chosen by welcoming our new surroundings and absorbing the brand new atmosphere. Adapting into the new is a very exciting experience because it is a different kind of change and is exactly what life experience is all about.

Let the Four Aces of Appreciation, Acceptance, Adjustment, and Adaptation marinate for a little bit. Once we grasp this concept, we are ready to go through our upcoming life experience with a little more ease. Remember, this is an ongoing process and each time you live a new experience, the Four Aces will come into play. You were dealt a good hand, so play your cards right.

"THANKS TO THOSE WHO HATED ME,
YOU MADE ME A STRONGER PERSON.
THANKS TO THOSE WHO LOVED ME,
YOU MADE MY HEART GROW FONDER.
THANKS TO THOSE WHO ENVIED ME,
YOU MADE MY SELF ESTEEM GROW STRONGER.
THANKS TO THOSE WHO CARED,
YOU MADE ME FEEL IMPORTANT.
THANKS TO THOSE TO ENTERED MY LIFE,
YOU MADE ME WHO I AM TODAY.
THANKS TO THOSE WHO LEFT,
YOU SHOWED ME THAT NOTHING LASTS FOREVER.
THANKS TO THOSE WHO STAYED,
YOU SHOWED ME THE TRUE MEANING OF FRIENDSHIP."

- UNKNOWN

Life Is Not a Game, Or Is It?

We move and eliminate people in our lives like pieces on a chess board. We roll the dice in life with hopes of landing on Park Place like in Monopoly. We take the risk of going all in with Pocket Rockets (2 Aces) at the Texas Hold'Em table. So why not see life as a game?

The life experience process is most similar to that of a Nintendo game after each level. The next level becomes harder, the enemies multiply and are tougher to kill, and the final villain at the end becomes harder and trickier to defeat. Throughout life, there should always be an incentive to continue, a light at the end of the tunnel if we must call it, and in video games, there is always an incentive to complete the game. There is always a goal to reach, but there are obstacles in between that we must experience and overcome and increase in difficulty with each new level. With every new level, we also gain more strength and knowledge for the next tasks we will face. But even if we die in the process, we still have the choice to start over and continue. If you ask me, it seems as if video games always had the right idea for what is life about, we just never put it into a deeper perspective.

The Hero's Journey

Let us examine the popular Nintendo game, Super Mario, on its perspective of life. (If you are not familiar with this game, then you definitely need to experience much more than you think!) The journey for Super Mario is a great example of how life should be experienced and how the process occurs. Come on, let's be honest, who doesn't want to run around like a maniac, break things with our heads, kill stuff with fire balls, eat mushrooms to get stronger, collect money, and make out with a princess at the end!? You see, Mario was a goddamn nobody. He was a simple Italian plumber with nothing to look forward to in life besides cleaning up the over flowing s#@t, unclogging the sewer pipes. But Mario knew there was much more to life than just being a plumber. He knew his inner talents were much more valuable aside from being swift with a plunger. Mario knew he had a calling to become something great and live life in a much bigger way. He just did not have the opportunity yet to become amazing. All of the sudden, Bowser comes along, casts a spell on the Mushroom Kingdom and kidnaps the Mushroom King's daughter, Princess Toadstool. (Her name gives her no justice, she was smoking hot!) As Mario is cleaning the toilets of disgusting excrement inside the Kingdom, he notices that the Kingdom needs help removing a spell and has a princess being held hostage. Mario is quick to realize that this is his chance to do something amazing and experience a journey he believed in. He is confident and ready to step into the unknown, bravely accepting the challenge that life has placed in front of him. This was his calling, his time to shine. Mario knew he was far more than a Ginzo plumber who fixes toilets. He knew was much more than just Mario. Instead, he was SUPER MARIO.

Super Mario's journey consisted of different stages in each level. In each stage, Mario faced different enemies and had to kill them with different attacks. He ate mushrooms to become bigger and stronger, ate flowers to throw fireballs, collected leaves to fly, played the flute to travel, collected coins to fill his pockets, and through all of his experiences, he stuck to the main goal of success:

To free his loved one, Princess Toadstool, and live happily ever after. Along the way, he faced many enemies who tried to stop him in his quest. These enemies included the Goombas, the Koopa Troopas, the Buzzy Beetles, the Bullet Bills, the Hammer Bros, the Jumping Cheep-Cheeps , and of course, the head honcho, Bowser. Whew! As you can see, there were a lot of battles Mario had to take on between attacking the enemies. Breaking blocks, jumping over bridges, collecting money, and who knows what else. (Talk about doing a lot of cardio!) Super Mario learned many new lessons throughout his quest such as overcoming innumerous amounts of obstacles, receiving guidance from others, and collecting power ups as he went along. Even when he "died" he still had the choice to continue his quest or start over. Either way, he decided to keep moving forward in his adventure. After all was said and done, Super Mario passed all the obstacles, killed all the enemies, defeated Bowser, and saved (banged) the Princess. He then chose to return back to the Mushroom Kingdom until his next adventure because that is what heroes do. Heroes live for the experience, live for the adventure, and live to explore new things on the journey.

This is the hero's journey and in one way or another, we are all heroes. To be the hero in our adventure we must accept the challenge to become greater than we think we are. We must continue to move forward with each experience so we can progress with the goals we have set within our hearts. We must live each experience with confidence, happiness, and enjoy each moment. The hero's journey is the utmost exciting experience we will ever encounter. During the hero's journey, the concept is all the same. From Super Mario to Luke Skywalker, Bo Jackson to Michael Jordan, and Wolverine to Superman, the end goal is always the same and can be seen in three different ways.

- **Separation**—We are first in a place of comfort but when reality sinks in, we choose to leave and courageously step into the unknown. The separation process helps us face our fears by taking the initiative to proceed in what we believe. This is our call to adventure, our call to face new challenges.

- **Initiation**—Often, we are placed into a different spectrum to experience a particular voyage we have never witnessed. We physically enter the unknown with the risk of either losing or gaining. The initiation process will help us grow physically, mentally, and become more knowledgeable about life. We learn to overcome the fears that have held us back for far too long and accomplish the goals set in our hearts.

- **Return**—We come back from our quest (if we did not literally die) and share the stories of our triumph. We spread the knowledge gained and guide others on their own journeys because we have already fought the demons inside and have returned victorious. We have returned better, stronger, more satisfied, and more successful in pushing through all those scary things we once feared.

Remember, we all have our own paths in life. It is up to us to accept what have been placed in front of us. Even though the concept is the same, we all have a different purpose and we will all be a part of a different experience. Let us be the heroes of our own journeys by igniting the fires in our hearts, taking action on the thoughts that bring uncontrollable tears of joy to our eyes, and put

ourselves at risk in order to achieve the thoughts that
turn our stomachs into knots. Become the hero of your
life journey and experience the adventure. We all have a
choice to be something amazing and experience our own
hero's path. So when the opportunity of a new journey
presents itself, we can choose to either:

A) Be a victim of our own lives and blame everything
and everyone, including ourselves, for why we
cannot experience the journey.

B) Put our journeys in the hands of others and watch
them experience the life we envisioned.

C) Be responsible for our own adventures by moving
forward with the opportunity, regardless of what
might stand in our way. This is choosing to experience the Hero's journey.

What will you chose?

Finding Your Bliss

Our journey is not about what happens to us, it
is what we do with it when we return. It is always better
to have a story to experience rather than an explanation
or excuse. The journey we placed in front of us is about
exploring the new, sharing the acquired knowledge with
others, and letting all the emotions that come with it run
through our veins. It is about enjoying the process of going to places unknown and expanding our minds through
the eyes of others and different atmospheres. It is about
finding our bliss.

Once we are "successful", life becomes much harder than we expected it to be. New things happen that we
never believed could. Life changes at the blink of an eye
and it can go for the better or for the worse. It is easy to get

lost in the light of success because it happens at blinding speed and flashes away before our eyes can adjust. After we accomplish "success", many people get caught up in the material world and believe they will be happy. Our lives have changed for the better and so has our bank account. We choose to purchase materialistic things because we can. Now, I am not trying to contradict or say the opposite, because material items and expensive experiences are nice to have. But do they have a true meaning? Without a meaning behind the material success, they are just "things" and not a symbol of true happiness. Having material items are only a small part of our success and will only add just a little pizzazz to our joy. We unwillingly forget that our journey must also include good health and joy. Often, materialism makes us lose touch with our inner selves and we choose to "match" our happiness with the purchase of expensive jewelry, clothing, electronics, nice cars, and alcohol because this is the atmosphere we grew up around. We have been brainwashed to believe that these items will bring us true happiness. We choose to purchase a 90" screen TV only to become more hypnotized by the fluff the generation of today shoves in our faces. Think about it, what purpose does a super-sized flat screen TV do for us besides max out our credit card? Nothing. If compulsive shopping was not enough, we also choose to go out and drink ourselves into a mess, shove our faces with drugs or other garbage, and f#$k anything with two legs. These actions are not ones of happiness. They are examples of behavior, a celebration of gluttony. When the "celebration" is over, we are left emptier than the bottle of vodka we downed the night before with the two floozies lying next to us. Is this quite an experience? Yes, but it is not a passionate nor genuine one. Losing ourselves among the materialistic world is not healthy, wealthy, joyful, or even remotely the meaning of happiness. It is certainly not our bliss.

In conclusion, what is it that we are truly passionate about? What is that one thing we cannot stop thinking about no matter how hard we try? What is it that brings a little spark of madness inside our souls? The answer to all those questions is what we should be doing more of. After the success we achieve, we should experience the life that we cannot stop thinking about. Experience what brings the joy to your heart and to the people you love. Spread your success and happiness so that you can enhance the world and those around us. The journey of life is not about experiencing what we want, it is about experiencing what we love and being truly at ease with ourselves. It is about enjoying the moment of being ourselves and absorbing all the beauty this world offers to our senses. It is about appreciating what has become of us and how we spread our love within and without, just f@#$ing loving life. If you find all of that, you have found your bliss.

"We may get lost during our search of finding our purpose in life, but we are not truly lost. For our purpose in life is to simply live." —Jerome "Jay" Isip

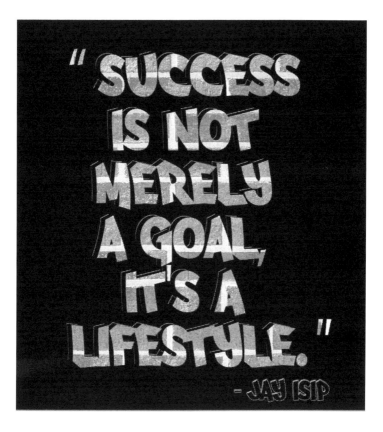

References

"average joe". n.d. Web.Wikipedia, the free encyclopedia. July 2014. <www.wikipedia.com>.

"dickhead 2a.". 14 March 2003. Web. UrbanDictionary. April 2014. <www.urbandictionary.com>.

"diddlysquat 2.". 28 August 2008. Web. UrbanDictionary. August 2014. <www.urbandictionary.com>.

"fluff 4.". 25 June 2006. Web. UrbanDictionary. July 2014. <www.urbandictionary.com>.

"fugazi 1.". 5 May 2003. Web. UrbanDictionary. July 2014. <www.urbandictionary.com>.

"golden shower 1.". 12 December 2003. Web.UrbanDictionary. April 2014. <www.urbrandictionary.com>.

"James Truslow Adams: American dream". n.d. Web. Wikipedia,the free encyclopedia. July 2014. <www.wikipedia.com>.

"mollies". n.d. Web.Wikipedia,the free encyclopedia. July 2014. <www.wikipedia.com>.

"pansy 5.". 30 October 2006. Web.UrbanDictionary. August 2014. <www.urbandictionary.com>.

"rounders 1.". 28 October 2004. Web.UrbanDicationary. April 2014. <www.urbandictionary.com>.

Boiler Room. Perf. Ben Affleck. 2000. Film.

Byrne, Rhonda. *The Secret*. Atria Books/Beyond Words, 2006. Hardcover.

Centers of Disease Control and Prevention. *Fact Sheets - Alchohol Use and Your Heath*. n.d. Web. August 2014. <www.cdc.gov>.

Cialdini, Robert B. *Influece: The Psychology of Persuasion*. Revised. Harper Business, 2006.

colossus of clout 1. 11 April 2011. Web.UrbanDictionary. June 2014. <www.urbandictionary.com>.

Deep, Mobb. "Shook Ones." *The Infamous.* 1995.

Effective action. n.d. Web. Wikipedia, the free encyclopedia. May 2014. <www.wikipedia.com>.

Electric charge. n.d. Wikipedia, the free encyclopedia. May 2014. <www.wikipedia.com>.

Finding Joe. Dir. Patrick Takaya Solomon. Prods. Patricia Fraizer and Patrick Takaya Solomon. 2011. DVD.

GodVine. *Basic English Translation (BBE) Timothy 6:10.* n.d. Online Bible. April 2014. <www.godvine.com>.

Luciano, Charles "Lucky". *Search Quotes.* n.d. Web. April 2014. <www.searchquotes.com>.

Napolean Hil Foundation. "Thought of the Day." 5 June 2014. Email Subscription.

Napolean Hill Foundation. "Thought of the Day." *effective action.* n.d. Email Subscription. 1 July 2014.

Newton's laws of motion. n.d. Web.Wikipedia, the free encyclopedia. May 2014. <www.wikipedia.com>.

Positive mental attitude. n.d. Web.Wikipedia, the free encyclopedia. May 2014.

Proctor Gallagher Institute. *The Science of Getting Rich Event.* Los Angeles, CA, 2014. Seminar.

—. *The Science of Getting Rich Event.* Dallas, TX, 2014. Seminar.

Rovio Entertainment. "Reports 2013 Financial Results." n.d. Web. August 2014. <www.rovio.com>.

Sour diesel. n.d. Web.Wikipedia, the free encyclopedia. May 2014. <www.wikipedia.com>.

SPIKE. *THE TOP 10 CRAZY BASTARDS WHO ACTUALLY CHANGED THE WORLD (FOR THE BETTER).* 02 October 2009. Web. August 2014. <www.spike.com>.

Terrelonge, Zen. *Angry Birds: The Mobile Entertainment.* 21 January 2014. Article. 2014.

The Business of Mobile Content. *Angry Birds: PG Connect: Rovio's Vesterbacka:They called me crazy- now Angry Birds rivals Coke.* 21 January 2014. Web. August 2014. <www.mobile-ent.biz>.

Wattles, Wallace D. *The Science of Getting Rich.* Trans. Bob Proctor. Revised. LifeSuccess Productions,

1996,2003,2007. Book.

Wing, Rev. Charles S. *Story of the Engine that Thought It Could.* 8 April 1906. Wikipedia, the free encyclopedia. June 2014.

Wiseman, Richard. *Self help: forget positive thinking, try positive action.* 30 June 2012. Article. May 2014. <www.theguardian.com>.

Printed in Great Britain
by Amazon.co.uk, Ltd.,
Marston Gate.